Rural Community History from

Trade Directories

by

Dennis R. Mills

A LOCAL POPULATION STUDIES SUPPLEMENT

Published in 2001 by
LOCAL POPULATION STUDIES
Aldenham, Hertfordshire

© Local Population Studies
Department of Humanities, University of Hertfordshire,
Hertfordshire WD2 8AT

ISBN 0 9503951 9 6

*The publication of this volume has been
assisted by an award from the
Marc Fitch Fund,
which is gratefully acknowledged.*

Typeset by Fort Services, Cambridge
Printed in Great Britain

CONTENTS

CONTENTS

LIST OF TABLES

LIST OF FIGURES

PREFACE

Apart from the publications by Shaw and associates, which were mainly written for professional use in urban contexts, there is no general work on trade directories. In this respect they are unlike many other great classes of historical source material, such as the census enumerators' books, wills and inventories, maps, land tax assessments, enclosure and tithe awards, and parish registers, which have whole bodies of literature devoted to their interpretation and use. Nor have family historians sought to include directories in their booklet series, although other documents are well covered from their point of view. Directories have fallen into this limbo partly because they appear to be straightforward to use (this is not so, although they are less problematical than many sources), and partly because they are printed sources, whereas the other great classes of source material are nearly all in manuscript form.

This book sets out to fill the space so identified and to expand very considerably the brief treatments given to directories in the many general introductions to local and community history. It is aimed at the beginner without a formal training in the field, but can also be useful to many with such an advantage, especially students wishing to base a project on relatively easily available source materials for rural community history.

Many of my Open University students did projects based on directories, work which prompted me to write this book. I should also like to acknowledge the help and encouragement of Marjorie Andrews, Alan Armstrong, Catherine Crompton, Colin Hayfield, Mary Hodges, Jennifer Jackson, Elaine Johnson, Chris Lester, Bernard Madden, Joan Mills, Gareth Shaw, Ken and Margaret Smith, Judy Willis and Matthew Woollard. In a special category is Nigel Goose, editor of *Local Population Studies*, who made a special journey from St Albans to faraway Lincolnshire to discuss the book and its illustrations. Any remaining blemishes are mine.

Publication of this book has been facilitated by an award from the Marc Fitch Fund, and I would like to express my gratitude to Roy Stephens and to the Fund for their support.

Dennis Mills, June 2001

CHAPTER ONE

INTRODUCTION

The traditional village was also a face-to-face society, in which persons knew each other in more than one role – or rather knew each other as persons as well as actors in particular roles; social relations were therefore characteristically 'many-stranded'. – Obelkevich, *Religion and rural society*, 24.

Community history

'Community' is an overworked word, used in a bewildering array of contexts — 'the international community', 'care in the community', 'the Catholic/Protestant/Jewish community', 'the farming community', and so on. Historians who use the word must therefore proceed with caution.

'Community' is introduced here as an adjective for a number of reasons. Firstly, 'community history' is preferred to the more conventional 'local history' in order to mark a deliberate emphasis on people, rather than on places. Although 'community' often, even usually, implies place, the chief concern is nevertheless with people, with relationships, and not just among 'important' people, but among as large a proportion of the population as evidence permits.

Secondly, the study of population is an important ingredient of 'community history': the rise and fall in population and the varying population sizes of rural communities are seen as crucial starting points. Life in a village of, say, 1,000 people was significantly different from life in a hamlet of 100 people, or in a lonely farmstead containing a dozen family members, labourers and servants. Rapidly expanding youthful populations were different from declining and ageing populations, and so on.

Thirdly, 'community' is used in the sense of a face-to-face community, a population small enough for most or many people to have been known to each other in the days when work, school, worship, play and shopping frequently went on for many people in only one place (Fig. 1.1). Even when they lived in isolated hamlets and farmsteads, rather than in a nucleated village, these factors would enable them to maintain a wide range of face-to-face contacts. Conveniently, 'community' in this sense is broadly synonymous with the smallest administrative units of township and parish. Relationships *within* these communities, such as who exerted power over the others, who were employers and employed, who worshipped together, and so on, are of interest to community historians.

Fourthly, there were important relationships *between* face-to-face communities, illustrated, for example, by farmers going to market and servants to

Fig. 1.1. Deanshanger (Northants), fete on the village green, 4 September 1937: an example of a community activity. Mr Comerford's ice cream van always came out from Northampton for this annual event. (Source: Deanshanger Village Heritage Society).

hiring fairs, swains looking for sweethearts, tradesmen for customers, patients for doctors. The life of the countryside was tied into that of the market towns, themselves often not larger than overgrown villages. But more than that, there were important contacts between neighbouring villages, especially between large villages and small, the latter dependent on the former for many services. Even places of similar size might be drawn together by sharing service outlets.

Fifthly, it follows that some communities were not simply territorial. A nonconformist congregation residing in a wide scattering of villages might be regarded as a distinct community maintaining its face-to-face relationships through the Sunday gatherings. These were not purely religious occasions, but also opportunities for business deals to be struck, marriage partners found, and the latest political issues to be debated. Such communities overlapped and co-existed with the more strictly territorial communities. Many people lived, as today, in more than one community at once.

Finally, agriculture was, of course, the basis of the rural economy except in a relatively small proportion of villages where mining and manufacturing were important. Despite the disappearance of the common-field system, in some respects farm work was still a communal activity (Figs. 1.2–1.3).

Trade directories

For the community historian, trade directories are the most accessible of the relevant sources of information. Directories providing a comprehensive

Fig. 1.2. Norfolk women harvesters about 1900 photographed by Viola Grimes of Castleacre. Farming was very labour intensive, especially on this farm where the reaper-binder had not been adopted. Although a horse-drawn reaping machine was in use, women were still employed to bind the corn into sheaves. The machine can just be seen in the centre of the photograph, and men are at work putting sheaves into shocks or stouks to speed up the drying process. (Source: Norfolk Library and Information Services).

coverage of the countryside were published at the rate of about two or three a decade from c.1840 to c.1940. The recent popularity of family history has made them expensive books, but many public libraries, especially central libraries, have a good stock for their county or locality.[1] It is usually possible to have entries for individual parishes photocopied at relatively little cost. Many county record offices are also equipped with a good selection, sometimes for counties other than the county in which an office is located. Modern reprints are available for a few directories. In recent years a few directories have been published on CD-Rom and probably on the internet — enquire through the relevant county or local family history society.

Most directories begin with a general section on the whole county or district, comprising topographical and historical information, as well as lists of areas, places or persons of significance in particular contexts, such as country seats with their occupiers, justices of the peace, and statements regarding administrative areas, such as the old hundreds and wapentakes, and the Poor Law Unions set up after the 1834 Poor Law Amendment Act.

Before approximately 1860 many of the directory editors except Kelly used the hundreds or wapentakes as a way of ordering parish entries. In these cases

11

Fig. 1.3. Men thrashing at Branston (Lincs), early twentieth century. Use of steam-thrashing sets required more men than the regular workforce of many farms. The boy on the left looks far too smart to have been working in the 'chaff-hole'. Thrashing was a social occasion, the farmer's wife providing food and plenty of drink two or three times during the day. This set probably belonged to the Forman brothers, who operated from an old quarry as agricultural machinery contractors, later a haulage firm. This was sold in 1985 and the quarry is now a housing estate. (Source: Branston History Group).

one finds brief introductions at the beginning of each hundred, and this layout means the reader has to make considerable use of the index in order to find particular places. This need was reduced by the adoption of Kelly's A–Z system of listing places, but for small villages and hamlets the index is still often a very necessary tool, since such places are frequently listed with their larger neighbours, although some have cross-references at their appropriate alphabetical positions.

Each entry for a parish in a trade directory has two sections (Fig. 1.4):

The parish description, which includes topographical, historical and institutional information; these descriptions are discussed in Chapter 10.

Lists of gentry and clergy, farmers, and tradesmen and craftsmen; such lists can be used as the raw material to discover commercial relationships both within and between rural communities and are discussed in the middle chapters of the book.

Following the A–Z place listing, there are often county lists of 'private residents' and lists for each trade and profession (see Chapter 9). The latter are

BELTON is a small township, in the northern division of the county, hundred of West Goscote, rural deanery of West Akeley, Loughborough union and County Court district, 4 miles N.W. from Swannington station, 3½ from Whitwick station, 5 from Castle Donington, 6 W.N.W. from Loughborough, 5 N.E. from Ashby, and 123 from London. St. John the Baptist's Church is a handsome, Early English building, comprising chancel, nave, aisles, and tower (in which are three bells), surmounted by a lofty and elegant spire. In 1877 some judicious restorations were effected at a cost of about £300, which was chiefly defrayed by the patron. The chancel door was renovated and removed nearer the communion rails, the floor relaid with encaustic tiles, a new reredos supplied, a stained east window, representing John the Baptist (by Heaton and Butler), inserted, and an ancient tomb of the foundress removed from the east to the west end of the church. The font was also removed and renovated, a large portion from the stonework refaced, and the tracery of several windows (including four in the tower) renewed. There are four arches on each side of the nave, supported by octagonal columns, with carved capitals. The oaken chancel roof is supported by richly moulded corbels. The chancel window and the oak screen which separates the chancel from the nave are in the Perpendicular style. There are two piscina and a niche on the north side, probably used as a credence table. There are some monumental tablets and tombstones to the Toone family. The Register dates from 1538. The living is a vicarage of the yearly value of £180, with residence, in the gift of W. B. Buddicom, Esq. There is a good National School, also a Wesleyan and a Baptist Chapel. There was formerly a market here. A horse fair is still held on the second Monday after Trinity Sunday. The inhabitants have the benefit of Shaw's charity of £8 a year for clothing. The principal landowners are E. F. Dawson, Esq., lord of the manor, A. C. P. de Lisle and N. C. Curzon, Esqs. The acreage is about 1900 ; rateable value £4246 17s. 6d.; the population in 1881, including the liberty of Grace Dieu, 645.

In the liberty of Grace Dieu is situated the manor house and Roman Catholic Chapel, dedicated to St. Mary, in which service has not been held since Mr. de Lisle removed to Garendon park. The manor house is now the residence of E. J. Coope, Esq., J.P.

ST. JOHN BAPTIST'S CHURCH.—Services, Sunday, 10-45, and 3 in winter, 6-30 in summer. Communion first Sunday in month. Rev. J. E. Middleton, M.A. Wardens, Messrs. W. Toone and S. Shaw ; Organist, Miss Middleton ; Clk, Jno. Gibson. Hymns A. & M.

CHAPELS.—Wesleyan, services, Sunday 2-30 and 6. Steward, Charles Sutton.—Baptist, 2 and 6. William Dalby.

POST OFFICE.—Jno. Cufflin, receiver. Letters from Loughborough delivered about 9 a.m.; box cleared 4-30 p.m. week days only. The nearest Money Order and Telegraph Office is at Sheepshed.

Belton.

Allsopp Mrs. Mary
Gibson John, parish clerk, cowkpr, tailor and v, Queen's Head
Gough Edward, butcher
Hatton Mrs. Elizabeth, dressmaker
Hatton John, tailor
Middleton Rev. Jph. Empson, Verge
Shaw William, bha, Bull's Head
Sutton Joseph, cowkeeper
Toone William, brewer & maltster
Upton Thomas, wheelwright

BOOTMAKERS.

Roome James | Roome William
Shaw Samuel, and grazier

FARMERS AND GRAZIERS.

Bacon William | Barton Benjamin
Blunt William Hurst
Dalby William | Fowkes Owen
Green Joseph | Green Joseph, jun.
Mosley George | Mosley William
Sutton Joseph | Williamson John

GRAZIERS.

Barton Benjamin
Draper Joseph, and miller
Emerson John, and v, George Inn
Farmer Thomas, and blacksmith
Holloway George, & baker & grocer

GROCERS AND SHOPKEEPERS.

Cufflin John, and draper & assistant overseer, post office

Cufflin John, jun, and draper
Holloway George, & baker & grazier
White John

Grace Dieu.

Godfrey Mr.

FARMERS.

Baguley Thomas
Carter John, the Warren
Gilbert Thomas, Merill grange
Husbands William | Jesson Wm.
Johnson John, Hill Parks farm
Kidger William and Son (John)
Peat George, Low Wood

CARRIER.

King, through from Osgathorpe to Ashby, Th.

Fig. 1.4. Entry for Belton, C.N. Wright's *Directory of Leicestershire*, 1884, exemplifying the usual two sections. Following the geographical description, the first section contains an ample account of the recent church restoration, before moving on to ecclesiastical and other forms of administration. In the second section the lists are divided between Belton and the secondary settlement of Grace Dieu. An attempt has been made to classify the occupational entries. There are several examples of dual occupationists, of which more is said in Chapter 5.

especially valuable because they remind us of trades that have disappeared or changed out of all recognition. The number of entries found under particular headings give an immediate indication of how specialised or how general were particular trades. Thus Kelly's *Directory of Dorsetshire* for 1920 lists 18 motor car proprietors, but 60 carriers; 44 gamekeepers and their employers; and 16 gas companies and 5 electric light companies, to name but a few entries chosen randomly.

In using directories for historical research, bear in mind their origins. First and foremost, they were intended to appeal to those in commerce who needed to send goods and circulars out to persons of particular occupation and standing.

For example, an ironmonger in a country market town needed to know how to get, say, half a dozen new plough shares to a farmer in a particular parish. For this purpose he would use the carrier's cart, and the directory would tell him on which day or days this ran, and from which hostelry it set out. On sending out his bills, the ironmonger could use the directory for correct postal addresses, which for a significant number of outlying farms were different from the names of the parishes in which they were situated. Conversely, a countryman could look through a directory just as we look through the *Yellow Pages*, in order to find 'the man for the job'.

Similarly, poor law administrators, clergy, magistrates, solicitors and many others would find the directories useful in their conduct of public business. For example, parish clerks were usually listed and anyone needing information from the parish registers, perhaps in connection with applications for poor relief, would be able to refer to the directory. Prospective employers would be able to check the names and addresses of previous employers when filling vacant posts. The antiquarian would be alerted to places worth visiting, such as ruined abbeys or beautiful parish churches, especially perhaps those restored at great cost to persons named.

It is for these sorts of reason that the ordinary working man, let alone his wife, does not appear in directories. Instead, it can be said that most of those who were economically 'significant' appear, but they do not constitute the majority of householders. Some town directories were more comprehensive, which probably explains why White, in his 1863 *Directory of Leicestershire*, put a disclaimer at the head of the town entries: 'The following Alphabetical Directory contains the Addresses of all the Inhabitants, except Journeymen and Labourers...'.

How accurate were the lists is a matter for careful consideration, but the mode of collection of the information is approximately clear. In the preface to his 1856 *Directory of Lincolnshire*, William White claimed that the information was 'collected and verified by personal visits to every parish and almost every house'. In practice his agents would have relied a great deal on local worthies, such as overseers of the poor, who had rate books to refer to; or schoolmasters, clergy, constables, and others who kept lists of names for a variety of purposes. Claims are sometimes made that pressure was put on people to buy directories by implying that failure to do so would lead to the offending person being missed out of the next edition. There is some evidence of copying carelessly from one edition to another, even cribbing from another firm's directory. Kelly, who eventually had a near monopoly of directory publication, got postmen to circulate questionnaires and to sell directories until he was stopped from abusing his connection with the Post Office.[2] But this is unlikely to have completely eradicated the involvement of postmen, who could easily have been consulted locally by the agents who collected information.

Commercial directories first started to appear for urban areas in the second half of the eighteenth century. In the early nineteenth century, nearby villages would often be included and by the 1830s such directories were being published with county labels. However, despite its title, Pigot's Directory of Monmouthshire for 1835 is typical of this period in containing particulars of eight market towns of the county, but of only nine villages, with the exception that gentlemen's seats are mentioned over a wider territory.[3]

Therefore, only from about 1840 can one expect to find directory entries for most villages. From 1840 directories appeared every few years until the second world war brought a halt. After 1945 directory publishers reverted to the pre-1840 practice of covering urban areas only, sometimes adding a few nearby villages as before 1840. This means that there is only about a century of rural history, *c.*1840–*c.*1940, during which nearly all villages can be studied with the help of directories.

Topics on which directories are useful include:

Tracing family trees. This can only be done for the 'better off' elements in the population, but as directories are easy to search, not much time will be spent on checking. Look in neighbouring communities, as well as the place where you expect to find an ancestor's name. If the same surname turns up with a different Christian name you may have a clue to the family's whereabouts that can be followed up in census indexes and other sources.

Complementing information in the census enumerators' books. The most important point to make here is that in the census many men who had occupations such as wheelwright, blacksmith, grocer, and mason failed to state whether they were apprentices, journeymen or masters, even though enjoined to do so by the census authorities. In some cases the enumerator was possibly too lazy to copy these particulars from householder schedules to his enumerator's book. At any rate, it is reasonably certain that countrymen appearing in directory lists were all in business on their own account. The directories are also useful for cross-checking details such as spellings, and for filling out the picture of the community enumerated one-by-one in the census books.

Locating places of worship. There is a definite bias towards the Church of England establishment, so the names of rural deaneries are often given in the descriptive entries for individual places, but a mention of a Methodist circuit would be very unusual. Clergy of all denominations are listed, but there is usually far more information about an Anglican church, its patron and the living, than about any nonconformist chapel or Roman Catholic church. Nevertheless, for all denominations directories are excellent starting points, and sometimes the only information available on certain points, such as (re)building of nonconformist chapels at dates later than the 1851 census of religious worship.

Identifying occupiers of certain properties. This is not a common use because few premises are named other than country seats, but inns, public houses and even some named beer houses are consistently mentioned in connection with their occupiers' names. A few farms are named, usually the larger ones, and in big parishes there may be clues as to the location of their farms against farmers' names, for example, the names of hamlets, or distinctive areas, such as marshes or heaths.

Studying landed estates. Bias towards the establishment comes out again in this connection. In addition to appearing in lists of residents, the gentry and aristocracy often merit a mention in descriptive entries, and their ownership of land and the possession of the few remaining manorial rights are consistently noted. Some of their more important servants, such as estate stewards or agents, head gardeners, bailiffs in charge of home farms, and gamekeepers are usually listed. Even where they were not resident, their ownership of manorial rights and land is noted. If there is a list of several landowners' names not easily identified as gentry, sometimes followed by the phrase 'and other families', the reader should assume for the time being that landownership was much subdivided. Cross reference to the list of country seats in the opening pages of a directory enables most of the important landowners to be identified, but some will be resident outside the county concerned.

Relationships with nearby towns. The mention of carriers' services (and in the 1920s and 1930s sometimes bus services) and postal arrangements will indicate which towns provided higher order services for particular villages. In administrative fields such as poor law unions and postal services, one town will have had a monopoly, but as far as commerce is concerned we can assume that competition occurred, at least on the overlapping margins of the market areas of different towns. Directories are a good guide to the work of many authorities and organisations, such as co-operative societies, societies for the prosecution of felons, petty sessional divisions, rural sanitary authorities, in later decades the rural district councils, and so on. Information about such organisations can be found either under entries on individual townships, or under the appropriate town entry, or at the beginning of the directory in the general description of the county or district, or in earlier directories in the hundred or wapentake entry.

Tracing social services. In addition to what has been said in the previous paragraph, the entries for individual places may include information on local schools, friendly societies, and charities.

Transport and communications facilities. In addition to carriers and buses, directories give particulars of railway stations and canal wharves, long-distance waggons and horse-drawn omnibuses, and vehicles that met trains (usually provided by nearby inns). They also particularise the services provided in village post offices, for example, whether there was a money order service, a telegram service, or facilities for savings bank accounts. Later directories often give telephone numbers: the small proportion of householders with a 'phone even in the 1930s is quite striking to the modern eye, as is the large number of small exchanges, often operated by the village postmaster or mistress. Telephone directories were first published in the 1890s and some have been reprinted.

Maps in directories. Many directories were published with fold-out maps of variable accuracy tipped into the binding. Those surviving the rigours of long usage are worth looking at, as they will be relatively up-to-date in relation to the directory's date of publication — but try a few tests, such as dates of railway construction. The scales used mean that detail is limited, but the positions of railways, of turnpike routes through the marking of milestones, and of various boundaries could all be shown. Market towns might be identified, and the locations of New Poor Law workhouses indicated.

Studying crafts and services available at different dates. This is the major purpose of this book, so read on....

NOTES

1. A few libraries contain a copy of Shaw and Tipper, *Guide to directories*, which gives an almost complete listing of all directories published; there is also Norton, *Guide to directories before 1856*. Holdings vary a great deal from one major public library to another, and the numbers of directories published vary considerably between counties. It is worth asking if your library service has a listing: Herefordshire was able to supply the writer with such a list ahead of a visit to Hereford in 1979. As a published example see Tupling, *Lancashire directories*.

2. Norton, *Guide to directories before 1856*, 17–18; Shaw, *British directories*, 11; Shaw and Tipper, *Guide to directories*, 9–10, 22–3. Shaw and Tipper give the impression that 'the methods of obtaining information... usually involved either visiting houses, or sending or leaving circulars to be filled in by the householders'. This is probably a view of what happened in towns, and more so towards the end of the 'directory period'. For example, Mr J.W. Ruddock, whose firm published Lincoln City directories, remembered house-to-house canvasses of the city taking place between the wars. By employing a large army of temporary clerks, every effort was made to avoid omissions and double-counting by carrying out the canvasses in a few days. In country areas with their widely spread farming population, however, it seems more likely that a great deal of reliance was placed on local notables. It is evident, for example, that some of the topographical descriptions in White's *Lincolnshire Directories* for the village of Canwick came from a churchwarden who made similar notes in parish records.

3. Pigot's *Directory of Monmouthshire* for 1835, reissued by Brian Stevens, Monmouth, 1972. This is true of most, if not all, Pigot's directories. It is often better to choose a directory of the 1840s as a chronological starting point, as there was soon a rapid movement towards comprehensive rural cover by other publishers. Readers who wish to study the literature on the use of directories in urban areas are recommended to consult the items indicated in the bibliography by means of double asterisks.

CHAPTER TWO

TRADITIONAL TRADES AND CRAFTS

A craftsman is usually the designer of the thing he is making...A craftsman makes things by hand, one at a time, and can therefore impart an individuality to each product according to his or her own will. – Arnold, *Country crafts*, 47.

For some purposes it is useful to distinguish between those trades and crafts that existed mainly to serve agriculture, such as blacksmithing and wheelwrighting, and those that served the whole population, of which the retail shops and crafts such as tailoring and boot and shoemaking are good examples. How wide a range of crafts and trades was required to constitute the conventionally supposed 'self-sufficiency' of the village is discussed in Chapter 6. The present chapter considers some basic propositions first about crafts, then trades (insofar as these can be separated), followed by remarks on how enterprises were run, and finally the role of rural industries.

Crafts

Many traditional crafts went back to very early, perhaps even Roman, times and by the thirteenth and fourteenth centuries specialist craftsmen were numerous enough for their callings to be adopted as popular surnames. Some have survived in the usual spelling, others in archaic spellings. Examples include: Baker, Brewer, Brewster, Butcher, Cooper, Glasier, Mason, Miller, Plummer, Sadler, Slater, Smith, Taylor, Turner, Webster (weaver), and Wright. It is generally thought that these men had smallholdings for their own subsistence in the same way a priest had his glebe, and association with the land survived in many cases in Victorian and even later times. Some names of ancient crafts probably failed to become common surnames — joiner and shoemaker — whilst others developed after surnames had become completely hereditary, such as bricklayer, dressmaker, milliner, brasier, printer, clockmaker and builder. Likewise the distinctions between different kinds of smiths (black-, white-, tin-, and frame-) and wrights (wheel-, mill-, plough-, and ship-) appear to have come too late to be incorporated in surnames.)

In handling the usual single-word descriptions of crafts (and retail trades) listed in directories, it is important to consider how accurate and comprehensive these were. A craftsman's work may have been much wider than the description suggests (Fig. 2.1). For instance, it is very rare to find undertakers mentioned in directories, yet local enquiry will often reveal that village carpenters and joiners, who could make coffins, acted as undertakers. There was only an occasional need for this service, yet it was needed urgently when a death occurred, so the convenience of finding a man on the spot was

Fig. 2.1. John Thomas Chaloner's collar and harness maker's shop at Branston (Lincs), *c.*1920. Generally described as saddlers in the directories, there were Chaloners following this trade in the village from at least 1842 to about 1930, when the last of the line turned to the more modern trade of selling and repairing bicycles. The shop front was an ideal place for advertising, as this is the route passing through a long string of villages between Sleaford and Lincoln. In addition to horse collars and harness, bicycle wheels can be seen, and also what appear to be long, flexible drain or chimney-sweeping rods. The advertisements in the window refer to leather sundries, the plate on the left to Brasso metal polish, and above the window there are advertisements for a product made by F. Hopper and Co., called Torpedos (worming potions for horses?). (Source: Branston History Group).

Fig. 2.2. Joseph Kemp outside his ironmonger's shop at Collingham (Notts), probably just before the first world war. Many village enterprises changed hands rapidly, but the Kemps, like the Chaloners (Fig. 2.1), went through several generations in the same business. Apart from the obvious bicycles, with 28-inch wheels, the shop windows contained spades and sheep shears, a birdcage and a large clock, and the sign also appears to be in the form of a clock. (Source: Peter Morrell).

appreciated, as well as the fact that he would be known to the family. Bearers could be found on a similar basis and the sexton would dig the grave.

Thus a service that went unmentioned in the directory may nevertheless have been provided on a minor scale. Within the village 'everyone would know'. For example, even as late as 1971, when the writer went to live in the Nottinghamshire village of Collingham, enquiry in the shops for a supply of seed potatoes brought the response that I should go to Frank Bealby's. Mr Bealby was retired from a job in a Newark foundry, where he had gone to work after his father's wheelwright's business had been forced to close before the 1939–45 war. The Bealbys had 'always' supplied seed potatoes, which they originally collected from the railway station in carts sent there to dispatch new and repaired ploughs, a Bealby speciality. By 1971 the family had been dealing in seed potatoes for a century or more, and no advertising was necessary (see also Chapter 9 for more on this family).

So a conscious effort has to be made to think in generalist, rather than specialist terms. Although, as is shown in later chapters, there were many contacts between neighbouring villages, in the days when horse-drawn travel or shanks's pony were the norms there would be some reluctance to go out of one's village for everyday services and necessities. The railways probably made relatively little difference in this respect, being much more important for long-distance travel and for goods traffic. The coming of the bicycle at the end of the Victorian period must have been a fundamental factor leading to a change in attitudes, followed only 20–30 years later by the arrival of lorries, vans, cars and buses (Figs. 2.2 and 8.4).

An obvious manifestation of the relative lack of specialisation in the rural economy is the existence of dual occupations. Unable to get a full living from a single craft, many craftsmen combined this with small-scale farming, or with another often related craft, or with a retail trade. Such combinations were not by any means all recorded in directories, but good directories list enough to indicate their importance (see Chapter 5).

Another aspect of the generalist function of craftsmen is that they were producer-retailers or bespoke suppliers of goods. Thus the wheelwright would build a cart or waggon to suit an individual farmer and the land he farmed, much the same as the bespoke boot and shoemaker would measure his customers' feet. The bakers and butchers were more obviously producer-retailers, combining two functions which later became separated. There are now few suppliers of bread where baking is done by the same person or the same family on the same premises, and even fewer butchers' shops with their own slaughter-houses (Fig. 2.3).

Trades

The boundary line between the traditional craftsmen and tradesmen/retailers has to be somewhat arbitrary, which explains why readers will find the term trades/craftsmen frequently used in this book. Notice that the phrase 'learning a trade' applies to both of them equally. A few of the retail trades developed early enough for their names to be adopted as surnames, such as Chapman, Draper and Chandler, but others such as grocer, victualler and publican possibly arrived on the scene too late.

Whilst the tradesman's main function was retailing, his work often included an element of craft skill. For example, in the early part of the nineteenth century, inns and pubs still often brewed their own beer. In the case of the grocer, some materials would arrive in bulk and would require breaking down into retail portions by the grocer. Weighing out and packaging commodities such as flour, sugar and dried fruit, sometimes in front of customers, took up a lot of time and required a degree of skill if losses were not to be incurred. Similarly bacon and cheese were among the items that needed cutting up.

A grocery shop was often the basis for the sale of other articles, and a common combination was that of grocer and draper, although tailors were also sometimes drapers until they (the tailors) disappeared, often long before the end of the nineteenth century. The drapery side of the general store could be managed by a grocer's wife and she would not only sell materials for making up in the home, but also ready-made clothing and footwear as these became more easily available with the spread of the railway network.

Fig. 2.3. Alfred Goodyear's butcher's shop at Woodhall Spa (Lincs), c.1910s. The four staff had no fear of an environmental health officer telling them to put the carcasses into more hygienic storage! The butcher's cart on the left was an essential means of capturing the trade of many housewives living in isolated places. (Source: Maurice Hodson Post-Card Collection).

The general term shopkeeper poses the obvious question as to what the shop sold. It seems to have been used more in some directories and some districts than others, and is another indication not to take directory entries too literally. It seems likely that the 'shop' was a forerunner of the corner shop, or convenience store of the present day. If foodstuffs were the core of the business, to them could be added other day-to-day necessities, such as firewood, matches, candles, paraffin (for lamps), items for mending clothes, tobacco, and simple stationery items. Later would come newspapers and magazines, later still electric-light bulbs, and so on.

These generalities are supported by one of the examples reported in an article based on the accounts of Lucas Bemrose, a 62-acre owner-occupier farmer of Willoughby near Alford (Lincolnshire). [1] He made up his own directory for reference when he needed to buy something for the farm or the house. Under the name of John Sharp, given as a shopkeeper in White's 1862 directory, he recorded: agistment (hiring of pasture land), various types of animal feed, waggon/cart repairs, vegetables, bread, haberdashery and fabrics, hardware, carriage hiring, coal, groceries, meat, medicines, tobacco, pigs, and victualling!

Such a shop might also be a post office and to run a post office became, as now, a skilled job, requiring a good level of literacy and the understanding of bureaucratic rules somewhat foreign to Victorian villagers. Early directories generally only report letters being collected and delivered from the nearest post town at a certain person's house, once or twice a day. The growth of letter and parcel traffic required room for a minor sorting office from which the

Fig. 2.4. An enamelled metal plaque above Heighington (Lincs) post office window, photographed in 1993, erected about 100 years before, judging from directory entries. In 1896 this post office issued postal orders, but was not a money order or telegraph office. In 1900 a directory recorded that it was a 'Post and Money Order Office, Savings Bank and Annuity and Insurance Office', as appears on the plaque. (Source: D. R. Mills).

village postman could set out on his walk, probably twice a day, once only for outlying properties. In the 1850s and 1860s the Post Office began to extend the range of services offered, the first new service in most places being money order facilities. These appeared first in the towns, then in the bigger villages, working very gradually down to the smallest post offices over a period of 20–30 years. By the 1870s some village post offices had savings bank facilities, followed by the telegraph service perhaps in the 1880s and the issuing of annuity and insurance policies. Just before the First World War national insurance stamps came to be stocked and the associated old-age pensions were first paid out (Fig. 2.4).

By the 1920s, or a little earlier, the telephone appeared on the scene, manual exchanges being installed in rural post offices. Some of the latter also displayed adverts saying 'You may telephone from here', but soon this facility was transferred to public call boxes. In the 1930s the Post Office was also erecting the first automatic exchanges in rural areas, thus relieving postmasters of a tiresome 24-hour responsibility for connecting subscribers, and also incidentally giving greater privacy! Some of the early exchanges survive as elite garages and garden sheds, or with more esoteric functions such as village museum and doctor's surgery.

Another group of retail outlets requiring discussion are those concerned with the licensed or victualling trade. The term victualler was often used, referring

Fig. 2.5. The *Fox and Hounds* public house, Deanshanger (Northants), probably at the coronation of George V, 1910. In the days before village halls, pubs were even more important social centres than they are now. This group may have been a club of some kind, rather than the 'regulars' who happened to be present when the photographer paid his call. At any rate, apart from barmaids and landladies, pubs were still resolutely male-only territories. The *Fox and Hounds* was licensed to sell beer, spirits and tobacco, and belonged to the Brewery Company at Aylesbury, about 25 miles distant, and probably got its supplies by rail. (Source: Deanshanger Village Heritage Society).

essentially to alcoholic drinks consumed on or off the premises, but catering was also offered at the better-class establishments. These were the inns, which in principle were distinguished from mere public houses by providing meals and accommodation, and the changes of horses so vividly described by Dickens. Inns were also places where both formal and informal meetings took place, an example of the latter being between men who wished to strike business deals. In the days before schools and village halls, inns contained meeting rooms that were the only practical alternative to churches and chapels. Enclosure and tithe commissioners frequently met and held public meetings in inns. Auctioneers would conduct sales there. Even vestry meetings (the parish officers and ratepayers) would often 'adjourn' to a hostelry in preference to a cold church without refreshment.

With the decline of long and medium distance road travel, the inns also declined and many became inns only in name, providing only the simpler services of the pub — drink and limited forms of entertainment (Fig. 2.5). A third type of licensed premises were the beerhouses, established under the Sale of Beer Act (1830). They were limited to the sale of ale and beer, being unable to sell wines and spirits. They were the refuge of the working man, who was often glad to escape from an overcrowded and comfortless cottage into a slightly larger and warmer house. Beerhouses and beershops usually had no name, making them harder to trace in the directories. They seem to have been more common in some districts than others, possibly as a result of differing policies on the part of the licensing magistrates, who sometimes regarded them as dangerous hotbeds of political agitation, especially prior to about 1850. Beerhouses are unlikely to have often provided a full-time living — even inns and pubs were often kept by dual occupationists — and may have been mainly the province of working men's wives, despite the licences being in their husbands' names.

Although beerhouses and beershops were usually nameless, two studies have shown that they could be easier to trace in directories than in the census enumerators' books. In 1851 a directory listed 178 beer retailers in the borough of Bradford, whilst only 131 could be traced by various means in the census enumerators' books for the same year. A second exercise for 1891 showed that 22 out of a total of 287 beerhouses were 'missing' from the census. A similar study of the smaller town of St Albans (Hertfordshire) revealed a discrepancy between 13 beer retailers in the 1851 census and 35 in Kelly's directory of 1855.[2] It seems that even very minor commercial outlets would get included in a commercial directory, but might be eliminated from the census record in one of two ways: male heads of households might fail to include secondary occupations on their schedules, perhaps especially their wives' source of 'pin money'; and enumerators might have 'edited them out', encouraged in this by the official lack of careful attention to part-time and seasonal female occupations.

How were the enterprises run?

This question can only be answered in outline, as documentation, such as accounts and leases, is relatively rare. The capital required must have varied considerably from one trade or craft to another. The 'rough' carpenter who got a living mainly from setting up farmers' fences and gates and similar jobs would have needed a great deal less finance than a well-established wheelwright. It was usual for a wheelwright to have a stock of timber being seasoned in his yard, much of which he had selected and felled himself. As seasoning by traditional methods took several years, a considerable amount of capital would be locked up in this way. For example, when Joseph Moss, wheelwright of Collingham (Nottinghamshire), had his premises insured in 1887, his house was valued at £200 and the timber in his wood shed at £350, the whole property and contents being worth £735.[3]

The capital was often raised by inheritance, but the directories indicate that many trades/craftsmen did not stay in the same village for very long, suggesting that there was a class of more footloose men who had not inherited established businesses with extensive good will, whether in rented or owner-occupied premises. Journeymen often had their own sets of tools when working for other masters, so the minimum capital required consisted of enough money and/or credit to cover a year's rent of premises and some materials to start work on, and enough credit or cash to live on during the first few months of business. It is highly unlikely that banks had a significant role in the provision of credit to men so low in the social hierarchy lacking respectable sureties. There may have been men in the community willing to act as bank referees, but they were more likely to advance credit directly themselves.

In former centuries, before the days of pensions, retired men who had sold up their businesses would look for opportunities to lend money at interest. Perhaps remembering their own early days in trade, some would be willing to lend money to younger men starting out, although it is also well known that cottage property was a favourite investment in these circumstances. Men who had enough capital to 'own' premises on copyhold or freehold tenure could raise mortgages on this security, either to complete payment for the premises, or to provide themselves with some working capital. Dozens of such transactions were recorded, for example, in the Argentine and Trayles court books at Melbourn (Cambridgeshire), where copyhold was still a common tenure. Some men registered several mortgages over a period of 20–30 years, suggesting that they were continuously in debt for long periods.

Another avenue to be explored was the seeking out of suppliers who would supply materials on credit and this may have been particularly significant in relation to licensed houses tied to breweries. The village communities of the nineteenth century had an attitude to credit rather different from our own, partly because inflation was not a problem. Even as late as the 1940s some village blacksmiths only sent out bills once a year, traditionally in January, by which time farmers had thrashed a large proportion of the previous year's corn harvest.

There are also records and recollections of a semi-barter system of payments, whereby farmers would pay craftsmen partly in farm produce, and wheelwrights and blacksmiths (for example) would barter their respective products or services. Thus, when a cart wheel was to be re-tyred by the wheelwright, he would get the blacksmith to lend a hand as well as to provide the new metal tyre. In return, the wheelwright could supply, for example, new wooden handles for the many pieces of mainly metal equipment, like ploughs and seed drills, coming to the blacksmith for repair (Fig. 2.6). It is known that running accounts on a semi-barter, semi-monetary basis would go on continuously for years without being completely cleared. Those concerned were keen to cement working relationships within the community in such a way that key people owed them 'a good turn'. Economic relationships were intimately bound up with social relationships.[4]

Apprenticeship was an integral part of the traditional economy. Many crafts and some trades could not be entered without having served an appropriate apprenticeship, the typical period in a boy's life being from age 14 to 21. This tradition goes back far beyond the institution of formal schooling, so that many boys may have had only a basic grounding in literacy and numeracy. It is unlikely, however, that new apprentices were ever completely illiterate, since most trades and crafts demanded a reading and writing ability and some idea of accounts and calculations. Think of the carpenter's refined measurements and the trader's constant handling of measured amounts of many different commodities.

Fig. 2.6. Alfred Bielby outside his blacksmith's shop at North Grimston (Yorks, E.R., 1910s). The Bielbys were here for over a century and worked in close association with the wheelwright, only 60 yards away, who rolled his finished wheels down the slope to be tyred. In the picture to the right are some blacksmith's tools in a traditional box on legs, some of which would be sharpened on the grindstone (extreme left). Also on the left are items in for repair, including the wheels of seed drills or hay rakes, and some feeding troughs. Probably because the Bielbys ran a general store next door, the advertisements do not relate to blacksmithing, referring instead to Colman's Starch and Mustard, Thorley's Cattle Food and Lactifer for calves, and Scales and Sons best boots. (Source: Dr Colin Hayfield, and caption based partly on his 'Blacksmiths and blacksmiths' shops').

In return for his training the boy did some of the menial and less skilled jobs that characterised the Victorian shop or workshop: attention to heating and lighting, keeping the premises tidy, searching out and roughly preparing certain materials, holding the nervous cart-horse for the blacksmith and ladders for various kinds of craftsmen, running errands, and so on. Those who have looked at census enumerators' books will recall seeing that many apprentices lived with their masters, who were sometimes their fathers, but mostly were not. Apprenticeship was a social as well as an economic relationship, and the boy was expected to conform with 'house rules' in the same way as sons of the master.

The directories are silent on the numbers of apprentices and journeymen (waged workmen out of apprenticeship) employed by the masters whose names are listed. This is important in any consideration of the decline in rural trades and crafts. Thus masters' names might continue to appear long after they had ceased to employ journeymen or to take apprentices, who thereby suffered most from the earliest manifestations of decline. A middle-aged master would be reluctant to give up his self-employed status and might find it very difficult to pick up a new trade. The best course of action might often have been to cling on to the business on his own until 'retirement'.

Rural industries

So far the discussion in this chapter has concerned trades and crafts spread across the whole of the countryside very approximately in proportion to population. But there were also industrial crafts or domestic industries that were still important in the early Victorian period. These were not crafts in Arnold's sense of the term (see head of chapter) and they were relatively concentrated in particular districts, a process that had begun in the Middle Ages with the woollen industry in such specialist areas as East Anglia and the West Country. Although the towns were the centres from which this industry was organised, many workers lived in villages and hamlets partly because this allowed them to produce at least some of their own subsistence. Some processes also benefited from being located in country areas, strung out along watercourses that provided power for fulling and water for dyeing.

By the early nineteenth century water power, followed by steam, had brought domestic workers into spinning and weaving mills in the Pennines, where both water and coal were available in abundance. Such was the growth of the industry that erstwhile villages had swollen to the size of some market towns and the market towns had become great centres like Manchester and Leeds. A similar process, but at a slower pace, had been going on in the metal trades in areas like the Don Valley near Sheffield and in Birmingham and the Black Country. There were a few other areas in which water power and water itself were essential, leading to concentration as in the case of paper-making in south Hertfordshire and north Kent.

However, this still left many industrial workers using hand power in their homes or domestic workshops spread across many villages. Examples include footwear in Northamptonshire and Somerset, hand-knitting in the Yorkshire Dales, framework-knitting in the East Midlands, glove-making in Dorset, Oxfordshire, Somerset and Worcestershire, sailcloth-making in west Dorset, wooden products in the Furness district of Lancashire, lace-making in Buckinghamshire, straw-plaiting for the hat trade centred on Dunstable and Luton in Bedfordshire and St Albans in Hertfordshire, felt-making for hats in the Stockport area, chair-making in the Chilterns, basket-making where osiers could be grown, as in the Trent Valley north of Newark, and even the speciality of besom-making at Tadley in Hampshire.

The work was organised by men who lived in market towns, usually on the basis of country (and town) workmen and women going to the warehouse (sometimes called a factory) for materials, and returning them in a made-up state at the end of the week. The merchants or 'manufacturers' paid them by the piece and sold the finished products through wholesale connections up and down the country and overseas. The manufacturers appear in the directories, along with some middlemen who plied between them and the work people, but the work people themselves seldom appear there. This is because, although they worked at home out of sight of the manufacturers, sometimes using their own tools and hand-powered machines, they never owned the materials of their work and never came into contact with even the wholesale customer who bought the finished goods. They were workers, proletarians, not traditional master craftsmen, and of little interest to the people who made out of directories. In some industries different processes were carried out by different workers, only the last worker in the chain seeing the finished article. All the essential elements of modern industry were present except the use of non-human power that required the concentration of work in mills or factories.

Nevertheless, these industries are very important in the present context because they sustained rural populations at much higher levels than was possible where the only occupations were farming and its related crafts. Community structures were quite different: some villages contained several hundred female laceworkers, or male and female framework-knitters, or male chair bodgers. These numbers provided an enlarged market for the trades/ craftsmen in the traditional occupations supplying purely local needs. In the nineteenth century domestic workers often lived in penury, as their industries gradually declined in the face of urban, or foreign, competition. Their spending power as individuals was low, but their numbers helped to make up for this. What has been said of manufacturing industry can also be said of mining and quarrying activities, from tin and copper and china clay in Cornwall to lead-mining in the Pennines.

It is worth reading the directory entries for local market towns for evidence of the existence of domestic industries in your piece of the countryside.[5] Consult printed works of local history, one of the most useful of the widely available sources being the *Victoria County Histories* of individual counties, which often contain brief accounts of individual industries. If time permits, the census enumerators' books can be consulted to get a detailed overview of local occupations. The discussion of village population sizes is taken up again in the next chapter.

NOTES

1. Dixon, 'Lucas Bemrose'.
2. Jennings, 'Drink retailers', especially 31–2; Goose, 'Pubs, inns and beershops', 59.
3. Nottinghamshire Record Office, DDH 110/3.
4. Rose, *Good neighbours*, chapter V; Reed and Wells, Class, Conflict and Protest, 13–21, Mackelworth, 'Trades, crafts and credit'.
5. See, for example, Raven, 'Derbyshire'.

CHAPTER THREE

THE RURAL POPULATION

Rural depopulation has occurred in the past century and a half, and will
continue in the future, because of the declining employment opportunities in
the countryside.   – Saville, *Rural depopulation*, 7.

Trends

It has been suggested that community history should pay careful attention to
the study of population, including its age and sex structure, the sizes of
communities, overall trends in population numbers and employment
structure. Although there are various ways of separating urban and rural
populations, the main national trends, as shown in Table 3.1, are very clear. In
the early part of the nineteenth century (1801–41) rural population was
continuing the sharp increase that had developed in the last quarter of the
previous century, but because of an outflow to urban areas it was not keeping
up with the population increase in the country as a whole. Between 1841 and
1861, the early part of the Railway Age and the early years of the New Poor
Law, rural population was poised at about eight-and-a-quarter millions, the
peak from which it slowly sank until the end of the century. Ignoring the
hiccup caused by the extension of town boundaries in the 1920s, there was
then a slow, but steady recovery from 7.16 millions in 1901 to 8.44 millions in
1951. In the meantime, however, the population of the whole country had
continued to increase rapidly, so that in the 1930s country dwellers were
outnumbered by about five to one. (See Appendix 3.1 at the end of the chapter
on how to look up local population trends).

John Saville's forecast of 45 years ago (see chapter heading) proved to be
inaccurate, but rural population increases in the twentieth century have never
represented a real resurgence in the rural economy, since they have been due
to people with 'urban' jobs living in the country. Some have been townspeople
moving out, but many were, and are, country people who have left
agricultural and associated jobs, but are still living in their villages. Whilst
some services have been saved by these developments, in the
meantime changes in lifestyle, especially in mobility, in the age
structure of the population, and changes in the larger numbers and
turnover required to run, say, schools and village shops, have all
conspired to reduce service levels even in areas of expanding
population. In areas of absolute depopulation they have plummeted
downwards in a vicious spiral of cause and effect. In the last ten to
fifteen years or so there has been a big increase in the number of
people working from home by electronic means, but this trend seems
to have done little to stem the spate of closures of rural shops, banks,
pubs and other facilities.

Table 3.1 Population changes, England and Wales, 1801–1951

Census	England and Wales, millions	Eng & W, decadal increase %	Rural Eng & Wales, millions	Rural as % of Eng and Wales	Rural decadal change %	Rural percentage above 1801
1801	8.83		5.88	66.2		
1811	10.16	14.0	6.44	63.4	+9.5	9.5
1821	12.00	18.1	7.20	60.0	+11.7	22.3
1831	13.90	15.8	7.74	55.7	+7.6	21.6
1841	15.91	14.3	8.22	52.7	+6.2	39.7
1851	17.93	12.6	8.24	46.0	+0.2	40.1
1861	20.07	11.9	8.28	41.3	+0.5	40.8
1871	22.71	13.2	7.91	34.8	-4.5	34.5
1881	25.92	14.7	7.79	30.0	-1.5	32.5
1891	29.00	11.6	7.40	25.5	-5.0	25.8
1901	32.53	12.2	7.16	22.0	-3.3	21.6
1911	36.07	10.9	7.60	21.0	+6.2	29.2
1921	37.89	4.9	7.80	20.6	+2.7	32.7
1931	39.95	5.5	7.03*	17.6*	-9.9*	19.5
1939**	41.50		7.30	17.6		
1951	43.74	9.5***	8.44	19.3	+20.1***	43.5

Notes:
*   Affected by local government boundary changes, 1921-31.
**   National registration data. No census taken in 1941.
***   Based on change between 1931 and 1951.
          These censuses form the basis of the population figures given in directories.

Sources: reworked from Law

Many studies of the Victorian village set out to discover what village communities were like before these fundamental changes occurred in rural society, changing villages from communities dependent on agriculture to settlements inhabited largely by commuters. The average village was also transformed in much less than a hundred years from an essentially working-class community, in which farm labourers were much the biggest occupational group, to a predominantly middle-class community. In looking at the occupational structure of, say, 1892, the historian is making implicit comparisons with the present day situation, which is well enough known in

Fig. 3.1. Metheringham Heath School (Lincs), 1914. Gertrude (left) and Dorothy Ward with 31 pupils, probably the whole school. It served some of the isolated farming families of four heath parishes that met at the junction of what are now the A15 and B1202 roads. The youthfulness of the population is demonstrated by the fact that Metheringham parish had two other schools, one in the village and one at the fen hamlet of Tanvats. After the First World War the birth rate sank rapidly and this school closed long before the second war started. Its site is now marked only by the trees planted in the school garden. (Source: Mrs N. Troop, née Ward).

general terms. However, in the absence of directories and of suitable small area census data, local surveys are occasionally carried out to pinpoint the modern occupational structure.

One such survey is that for the Devon village of Widworthy, near Honiton, drawn up in 1992. Out of 204 persons on the electoral roll used as the basis of the survey, 16 had left by the survey date, 41 were housewives, 42 were retired, and 5 were unemployed, leaving 100 in gainful employment. Of these the quite large proportion of 16 per cent were engaged in agriculture, compared with 2 per cent of the national workforce and with the rough average of about 50 per cent across much of the Victorian countryside. Tourism accounted for 15 per cent of the 1992 workforce, a category almost non-existent a century before. Professional workers represented 18 per cent and a considerable proportion of the remainder were welfare service workers. A third of those in work were employed within the parish, a relatively high proportion for the 1990s.[1]

In the long period of decline the censuses show that rural communities became ageing communities compared to the vibrant towns. Nevertheless, down to about 1914 in relative terms there were many children in the rural population — perhaps one third of the total compared with about 20 per cent in more recent decades (Fig. 3.1). Conversely, the whole population has become much more elderly, so many Victorian villages had less than 10 per cent of their population in the over-65s, compared with about 25–30 per cent today. In the last century most villages had a preponderance of males, as there was a shortage of suitable work for women outside areas where domestic industries such as lace- and glove-making provided them with opportunities. This imbalance has since disappeared.

Large villages and small

In the modern media villages are almost invariably referred to as 'small', even when the population is measured in thousands. This kind of casual approach has to be avoided, since population size influenced many economic and social characteristics. In particular, size will have been an important determinant of the range of services that a village could sustain. A 1,000 strong population with perhaps 50 different trades was a very different community from the place that consisted of a few farmsteads, their attendant labourers' cottages, a vicarage, a post office and a pub. Not only were local trades and crafts concentrated disproportionately in the bigger villages but, in those districts where domestic industries survived, these also tended to be over-represented in the bigger villages.

Within a district sharing similar forms of farming — arable, sheep, dairying, beef cattle, fruit-growing, and so on — one of the most important factors influencing the size of the agricultural population was obviously the acreage. Mixed farming of the kind usual in lowland England needed about four men per 100 acres. A small, 1,000 acre township could, therefore, be cultivated by about 40 men. If they lived in, say, 25 households, the agricultural population would have amounted to about 25 x 5 = 125 persons. On this basis a 4,000 acre township would have supported about 500 people, a figure, as we shall see, much nearer thresholds required to provide a market big enough for a decent range of trades and crafts. This additional service population then took the total population to still higher levels, with progressively larger increments as different thresholds were passed. Getting to know something about township acreages is, therefore, an important early requirement (see Appendix 4.1).

But it is not just a simple matter of crudely estimating the size of the farm workforce. Quite apart from the importance of differences in soil fertility, the smaller townships were more likely to be dominated by large landowners than were the large ones and on the large estates the accent was on large farms with an efficient use of labour. Also, the size of the *resident* farm workforce was frequently smaller than the total workforce, owing to a policy of not providing cottages in the township for every labourer who worked within it. Men who attended stock were given priority, but many day labourers may have walked into the township each day from homes located outside it. These practices were especially common in the first half of the nineteenth century in the arable areas of south and east England, where the proportion of 'priority' workers was relatively low, and the proportion of casual labourers was especially high in the busy periods, notably the corn harvest.

Poor rates were an important consideration down to the mid-century, when Poor Law Unions gradually replaced the separate townships as the bodies with financial responsibility for the poor. The exclusion of casual workers from townships owned mainly by the big estates was a common device for restricting poor law expenditure. After the mid-century more estate cottages were sometimes built, but by this time the die of rural population distribution had been cast, and the general level of rural numbers was on its way down. Moreover, where a township contained a large gentry residence there was a tendency to restrict cottage building for social reasons — keeping out the rougher elements, making sure that game was undisturbed, and so on.

Large townships tended to exhibit opposite characteristics. Here there was more likely to be a significant number of small proprietors, hence also small farms, perhaps owner-occupied. In principle such holdings were less efficient in the use of labour, particularly when there were several growing sons and daughters at home. Wishing to have enough family labour on hand to cover the busiest periods, the smallholding farmer may have allowed his family to be underemployed in slack times, despite sending some of them out as casual labour on other men's farms.

In the larger villages there was a substantial body of tradesmen and craftsmen: publicans, blacksmiths, grocers, wheelwrights, millers, and so on. They were not a completely discrete element in the social structure, as many of them would have close links with the land. One example is the innkeeper, who kept a stable of horses for travellers, and would need pasture land and a supply of oats. Conversely, small farmers could use their holdings as a base from which to carry out a secondary occupation such as milling, malting, carting or providing a carrier service on market days. The farmers' buildings, produce, draught horses and vehicles could be used in different combinations for more than strictly farming purposes. All these activities were labour-intensive compared with general farming and contributed to the higher population density of the large townships and villages.

In such places there would also be builders who could run up terraces of labourers' cottages, some of which would be inhabited by men who worked outside their own townships at least part of the year. Most of these houses were owned by 'smock frock' landlords bent on making a profit from the rents. Building standards therefore had to be low, and unlike the estate cottages built for social reasons rather than for immediate profit, they have not survived in large numbers.

The distinctions drawn here between large and small villages are extremely crude. They apply more to the east and south of England than elsewhere. The object of these paragraphs has been to alert the reader to the existence of many reasons for keeping acreages and population sizes in mind when studying the information available in trade directories. The latter contain clues as to the social fabric in the descriptive entries for each village, for example, hints at the distribution of landownership. Villages with resident gentry are easy to spot and here the Church of England frequently had no competition from dissenting chapels. Larger places with one or more nonconformist chapels can be identified and provisionally assigned to the category where property was well sub-divided and sites could easily be found for chapels attended by small farmers and trades/craftsmen. Schools may have been provided by the aristocracy, gentry or upper clergy in many places, whilst in larger villages they sometimes had competition from nonconformist foundations (see also Chapter 10).

Appendix 3.1: Local population trends

An early task for community historians is to examine population figures for townships in their areas. Directories give the population of the smallest census units, usually a town, village or hamlet, at the last census for which information was available at the time of printing. To acquire a run of figures in this way is a tedious business, and sometimes the copying was inaccurate. A short cut is available in most counties in the form of the Table of Population printed in their *Victoria County History*, generally in volume II. Most of these tables cover the whole century from 1801 to 1901, but a few go beyond to various dates in the twentieth century. They also contain information on areas and boundary changes (see Appendix 4.1). Collections of population figures at the parish level during the twentieth century, especially the second half, will be found in large reference libraries in publications of planning departments; if these are not available, recourse can often be made to the individual census reports, which are found in larger numbers in public libraries than those for nineteenth-century censuses. By these means it is possible to discover local population trends to compare with the national trends shown in Table 3.1.

NOTE

1. Haydon, 'Recording history for the future'.

CHAPTER FOUR

CHOOSING COMMUNITIES

Billinghay, a large village on the navigable Car Dyke,...has in its township 1,462 inhabitants and 3,530 acres of land, including the scattered farms of Billinghay Dales and Fen.
Thorpe Tilney, a small village on an eminence,...has in its township 105 souls and 2,500 acres.   – White's *Directory of Lincolnshire*, 1856, 352 and 359.

General thoughts

For many readers the choice of a community will already have been made through interest aroused by residence or long association. Nevertheless, it is important to be aware of some of the implications of such a pre-existing choice, since the last chapter will have made plain that size of community will make a significant difference to the characteristics one is likely to encounter. Moreover, much deeper insights will be gained by placing the chosen community within a group of neighbouring communities with which it can be compared, at least on broad lines. It may be satisfactory for this purpose simply to take the ring of neighbouring townships, but similarity in soils and therefore farming is also important, and that might make the choice a little less straightforward. Farming was the foundation of most rural communities, so an effort should be made to understand its nature in your area.

General knowledge of the area may be sufficient to separate villages in a Pennine dale from those in the Vale of York; marsh villages from upland villages; Wealden villages from downland villages, and so on. The directories themselves are sometimes useful in mentioning the chief soil types and types of farming. For example, Kelly's 1881 *Directory of Nottinghamshire* is very specific in its description of Wollaton, now part of the city of Nottingham:

> The soil at the north end of the parish, clay, at the south end, sand; subsoil, at the north side, magnesian limestone, at the south side, fireclay and coal measures. The chief crops are wheat, barley, oats, beans, roots and hay.

Elsewhere it states that Lord Middleton's park extends to over 750 acres.

Such information should be combined with a study of those editions of Ordnance Survey maps which show relief features and parish boundaries — most of the One-Inch and Six-Inch maps, and the 1:25,000 maps (two-and-a-half inches to the mile). If a geological map can be found in the local library, so much the better. There are also useful reference books on the farming of most counties, especially those published in three spates, the first around 1800 when the Board of Agriculture published a series of county reports; the second in the

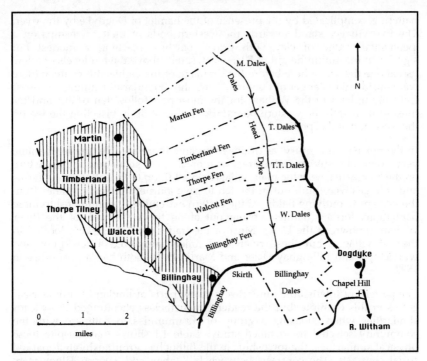

Fig. 4.1. Location map for townships in the Billinghay (Lincs) group. The hatched area is the 'peninsula' referred to in the text and the broken lines are township boundaries, where these do not follow watercourses. (Source: J. A. Mills).

middle of the nineteenth century when many counties were the subject of essays awarded prizes by the Royal Agricultural Society; and the third during the 1930s and 1940s when the Land Utilisation Survey published both One-Inch LUS maps and a series of county reports. It is also worth making friends with a knowledgeable farmer: most farmers have at least a nodding acquaintance with farming over a wide area, and often combine this with some knowledge of former farming practices. Field observations by the historian will help to corroborate and interpret much that is absorbed from other sources. Think about walking the township bounds and using footpaths to study the local types of farm land.

The Billinghay group of townships

To illustrate this section further, a group of five Lincolnshire fenside townships has been chosen, as seen in a map of the kind any reader might consider sketching on tracing paper with the help of OS maps (Fig. 4.1). Notice the similarities in the shapes of these townships, the fact of their all having the River Witham as their eastern boundary, and the narrow rectangles about four miles long set off from it. In the case of Billinghay the pattern is complicated by the presence of the hamlet of Dogdyke by the river. The five villages stand towards the western ends of their townships on a 'peninsular' ridge of clay with gravel patches, reaching a modest but significant maximum height of 50–60 feet, safely above the fen levels of a few feet above the sea, where before fen drainage of the eighteenth century there was considerable danger of flooding. Township boundaries running west-east from the upland to the Witham for the most part follow fen drains and for most of its length the western boundaries follow a drain bisecting the fen on the west side of the 'peninsula'.

In the nineteenth century, as drainage became more reliable, the fen became very predominantly an arable area, with most of the small amount of pasture on the 'peninsula' near the main villages. In addition to the latter, many farms and cottages were built out in the fen to save journeys of several miles from the villages to outlying fields. At the eastern extremity of each township these habitations formed hamlets strung out along the west bank of the River Witham, known as the Dales. Most of the trades/craftsmen were located in the old villages, but these riverside hamlets supported a few pubs and workshops, and Billinghay Dales and Martin Dales both had a post office in 1892.

The pattern of township boundaries in many parts of England is not as clear cut as in this example, but the reader is nonetheless encouraged to look for similarities when choosing a group of communities to compare with the community selected for detailed study. Table 4.1 shows that, despite these physical similarities, the townships in the Billinghay group exhibited marked social contrasts. The contrasts between Billinghay and Thorpe Tilney were especially strong, with the other three townships falling in between the extremes. Thorpe was the smallest township in terms of both acreage and population, but the enormous difference between it and Billinghay is brought out neatly by the population density figures: 49.7 persons per square mile in Thorpe Tilney, but over four-and-a-half times that level in Billinghay (230.7 ppsm). Over the nineteenth century Billinghay grew rapidly, Thorpe at a rate well below the national average.

Relationships between households in Thorpe Tilney must have been quite different from those in Billinghay. Thorpe could only sustain one type of service and a single service enterprise, that of a drainage engineer, who presumably served a much wider area than Thorpe itself. By contrast, Billinghay contained 42 different services in 1892, represented by 97 different trade/craft enterprises. Yet it had never been a market town, only a large central village offering services to other villages over a radius of several miles, where it was well able to compete with the more distant market towns of Lincoln, Sleaford and Horncastle. Among the trades/craftsmen were dual occupationists combining farming with other work: blacksmith, boat owner, hay and straw dealer, corn miller, potato dealer, auctioneer, timber dealer, agricultural machine owner, and grocer all figure in this way. This is a partial explanation of the average farm size of about 54 acres in Billinghay. At the other extreme was Thorpe Tilney with an average of about 480 acres, and the

Table 4.1 Billinghay group of townships, Lincolnshire

Variable	Martin	Timberland	Thorpe Tilney	Walcott	Billinghay
Area from White's *Directory*, 1856, acres	3632	2829	2500	3247	3530
Area from Victoria County History, acres	3777	2760	1929	3339	3671
(square miles)	(5.9)	(4.3)	(3.0)	(5.2)	(5.7)
Population 1891	777	443	149	531	1315
Pop. density 1891, persons per sq. ml.	131.7	103.0	49.7	102.1	230.7
Peak pop.	914	639	158	633	1501
(year)	(1871)	(1851)	(1871)	(1841)	(1871)
Peak % above 1801	201.7	78.5	65.6	75.3	159.2
No. of farms, 1892	27	24	4	26	68
Average farm size, acres	139.9	115.0	482.3	128.4	54.0
No. of services, 1892	19	12	1	12	42
No. of enterprises, 1892	44	18	1	17	97
No. of persons per enterprise, 1892	17.7	24.6	149.0	31.2	13.6

Notes: Average farm size has been calculated by dividing the number of farmers listed in the 1892 directory into the total township acreage. This introduces three relatively minor sources of error - the possibility of the directory omitting some small farms, especially holdings worked by dual occupationists; the unknown amount of overlap between farm and parish boundaries; and the inclusion of perhaps 100-200 acres of non-agricultural land in the total acreage.

Enterprises are counted under each of the trades/crafts followed by individuals; thus 'grocer, draper, and Post Office' has been counted as three enterprises, even though all were run by the same person.

Sources: *Victoria History of the County of Lincoln*, Vol II, Table of Population; White's *Directories of Lincolnshire*, 1856, 1892.

critical factor here was the near monopoly of landownership by the absentee landlord, Sir Thomas Whichcote, Bart.

Between these extremes, but resembling Billinghay more than Thorpe Tilney, was Martin (Fig. 4.2). Like many fen parishes its population had grown rapidly after the enclosure and drainage acts, with numerous small farms and other houses in the Dales and on the Witham Bank. In 1876 it got its own parish church, thus gaining independence from Timberland parish. This church was paid for substantially by the chief landowner, the Rev. J. W. King, whose ancestor Mary King gave money towards the building of the village school which still bears her name. Again the 1872 directory includes

TIMBERLAND PARISH.

MARTIN, anciently called *Merton*, is a large village, upon an eminence, on the west side of the Car Dyke navigation, 7 miles W. by N. of Tattershall, and 4 miles W. by S. of Kirkstead railway station. It is in Timberland parish, and its township contains 3632A. 1R. 17P. of land, mostly a low fen, extending five miles eastward to the river Witham, where there is a ferry to Kirkstead. Many scattered houses have been built on the banks and droves since the enclosure in 1789. It increased its population from 303, in 1801, to 914 in 1871. The Rev. J. W. King is lord of the manor, and owner of the greater part of the soil, the remainder of the land belonging to the Cartwright, Binks and Cawdron families. Here is a Wesleyan chapel, built in 1860 at a cost of £700, in lieu of the old one, erected in 1832, and also a Primitive Methodist chapel, built in 1837. Mrs. Mary King, in 1573, bequeathed two houses, with gardens, eight acres of land and a right of cutting turf on the fen, for the education of poor children of Martin. The Free school property now consists of a house, a schoolroom, barn, stable, 11A. 2R. 36P., in three closes, and an allotment of 22A. 2R. 2P., awarded at the enclosure. It is now let for £65 per annum, for which the master teaches all the poor children of the township. The school, rebuilt in 1842 and again in 1861, at an outlay of about £300, is used for Divine service, and attended by 50 children, who are under Government inspection. A good house for the teacher is attached.

Letter box cleared at 1.45 p.m.   Letters *via* Sleaford.   Billinghay is the nearest Money Order Office.

Andrews Samuel, bricklayer & buildr
Auckland Charles, farmer and victualler, Chaplin Arms
Auckland James, farmer, Fen
Baker John, seed merchant, Fen
Baldock Anthony, shoemaker
Binks Edmund Gilbert, Esq., Hall
Brown Edward, farmer, Dales
Burr George, farmer
Canham George, wheelwright and land surveyor
Cartwright Fowler, farmer, Dales; h *Abbey farm, Kirkstead*
Cawdron John, beerhouse & carrier
Cawdron William, farmer
Cawdron William, brewer & beerhs
Clay Thomas, farmer, Witham bank
Clifton Mrs Mary
Falkinder Charles, vict. Red Lion
Farbon Mrs Mary, farmer, corn miller and flour dealer
Farbon Robert, farmer
Fryer Francis (F. & Read)
Fryer & Read, blacksmiths
Gash Lumbley, farmer; h Thorpe Tilney
Gilbert Edward, shopkeeper, draper and licensed hawker
Goose Daniel, farmer
Goose James, farmer, Fen
Hansord William, shopkeeper, draper and shoemaker
Hawley Robert Stanley, master, Endowed school, rate collector, assistant overseer & land surveyor

Hawley Mrs Sarah Jane, mistress, Endowed school
Hicks John, blacksmith
Hollinshead James, corn miller, flour dealer and baker
Hollinshead James, farmer
Hollinshead Mrs Mary Ann, farmer
Holmes John, farmer, Moor
Howard John, farmer, Fen
Howard Sampson, farmer, Dales
Howard Thomas, farmer, Fen
Hufton Joseph, wheelwright
Idle Thomas, farmer, Fen
Kent Thomas, ferry owner and victualler, King's Arms, Dales
Knight Thomas, joiner, builder, brick, tile and drain pipe manufacturer & agent Royal Insce. Co.
Kyme William, farmer, Dales
Lawson Wm. plmbr. glazier & paintr
Lupton John, butcher and carrier
Marshall John, grocer, draper, coal dealer and vessel owner
Marshall John, butcher, shopkeeper and draper
Marshall Joseph, shopkeeper and draper, Dales
Marshall William, farmer, Fen
Newton Mrs Frances Isabella, day school
Newton Robert, grocer, tailor & drapr
Poole Robert, saddler & harness mkr
Read John (Fryer & R.)
Read Thomas, wheelwright
Revell John, farmer, Moor

Read William, shopkeeper & licensed hawker
Smalley Mrs Mary
Smalley Thomas, shopkeeper and licensed hawker
Smalley William, baker & shopkpr
Spencer William, farmer, Moor
Spicksley Richard & John, farmers, Moor
Sutterby John, farmer, Fen
Taylor James, tailor, Witham Bank
Taylor Thomas, shopkeeper and licensed hawker
Taylor Thomas, farmer, Dales; h *Kirkby-la-Thorpe*
Turner Richard Whitton, beerhouse, Dales
Tyler John, farmer, Dales; h *Linwood*
Ware Mrs Elizabeth, vessel owner
Webster Mr Cornelius William
Webster Joseph, farmer
Webster William, farmer
Webster William, farmer, Manor hs
Willson John, farmer, Fen
Wilson Mrs Susannah, boot and shoe maker, Dales
Wilson William, joiner & wheelwrgt

CARRIERS—To *Lincoln*, John Lupton, Wednesday and Friday; John Cawdron, on Friday only. *Sleaford*, J. Lupton and J. Cawdron, Monday

Fig. 4.2. Entry for Martin-in-Timberland, White's *Directory of Lincolnshire*, 1872. Another typical two-part entry like Fig. 1.4; see text for further comment. Compare with Fig. 5.1.

interesting examples of dual occupationists; some, like John Marshall, with an interest in river transport, still important despite the existence of a railway on the opposite bank of the Witham. Several of the shopkeepers were also licensed hawkers, which presumably assisted them in supplying isolated houses with a wide range of easily carried goods.

In Chapter 1 it was pointed out that there were important relationships between communities. So a detailed study of, say, Billinghay, would only make fuller sense if it included at least a broad comparison between that village and some of its neighbours. It had reached the size it was partly because of the growth of trades and crafts, a fact reflected in the ratio between population and trade/craft enterprises. In 1892 there were only 13 people *within* Billinghay itself to each enterprise, compared with 25–30 on average in Walcott and Timberland and about 18 in Martin. The Billinghay ratio also reflects the population that it served *outside* the village, whilst the generally small figures remind us that these enterprises were very small scale, mostly occupying one family. The ratio is also affected by the need for double counting of dual occupationists. The latter are the subject of the next chapter.

Appendix 4.1: Township acreages

These are almost invariably given in directories, but not always with great accuracy. Until the Ordnance Survey had carried out the surveying work for the first edition of Six-Inch maps, there was no one standard source in which acreages could be discovered. Earlier directories, therefore, relied upon a variety of individual sources, such as enclosure awards, tithe awards, estate surveys, rate books and so on, not all of which provided figures of tolerable accuracy. For instance, compare the figure of 2,500 acres given for Thorpe Tilney in the quotation from the 1856 directory at the head of this chapter and the figure of 1,929 quoted below. The tithe surveys were potentially the most reliable sources, but some townships contained land already free from tithe that did not come within the survey. The OS acreages include all roads and water bodies, which might take up 50–100 acres in the average township. The Ordnance Survey passed their figures on to the General Register Office for inclusion in the censuses, but it was only late in the century that all parts of the country were provided for in this respect, so any acreage in a directory published before that period needs to be confirmed. The easiest way to do this in most counties is to consult the *Victoria County History* Table of Population (see above, Appendix 3.1).

In some areas boundary changes occurred in the course of the nineteenth century, especially where urban and industrial change had been experienced. There is a reasonable prospect that such changes can be picked up from the footnotes in the Population Tables of the *Victoria County Histories*, or in the directories themselves. The latter are usually also quite explicit in explaining the differences on the ground between townships and parishes. The former were discrete entities for poor law purposes and in terms of open field farming, where that system of agriculture had prevailed. Many townships, especially in the south of England, were coterminous with ecclesiastical parishes, but in some areas of the Midlands and the north, where population levels had been low in the Middle Ages, it is often the case that a parish contained several townships. For example, referring to the Billinghay area, Billinghay parish contained the three townships of Billinghay, Dogdyke and Walcott; and Timberland parish the three townships of Timberland, Martin and Thorpe Tilney. Even townships might contain two or more separate hamlets, occasionally but not usually with identifiable boundaries within the township: in our Lincolnshire example the Dales hamlets did not have separate boundaries. All these matters should be sorted out at an early stage to achieve consistency in the handling of information.

An important consideration in rural areas is the density of population, since this places the relationship between acreage and population on a comparative basis. Wide differences within a group of neighbouring townships are often observed and can provide a starting point for investigations along the lines mentioned above. The quickest way of calculating density of population is to divide the acreage by the population at a given census. So at Thorpe Tilney in Lincolnshire where the acreage was 1,929 and in 1891 the population was 149 (Table 4.1), we divide 1,929 by 149 to arrive at a density of 12.1 acres per person. At nearby Billinghay no less than 1,315 people were settled on an area of 3,671 acres at an average of 2.8 acres per person.

However, if the acreage is expressed in square miles it is probably easier to grasp the way in which density varied. There being 640 acres in a square mile, it is necessary to divide this figure into the acreage to discover the area in square miles. The sum for Thorpe Tilney is 1,929 divided by 640 = 3.0 square miles. The density can then be expressed as 149 people divided by 3.0 = 49.7 persons per square mile. The calculation for Billinghay is 3,671 divided by 640 = 5.7 square miles. Division of the population of 1,315 by 5.7 yields a density of 230.7 persons per square mile. (See Table 4.1 for the other villages in the Lincolnshire example).

CHAPTER FIVE

DUAL OCCUPATIONS

The law required...that every waggon and cart bear its owner's name. One of the Roxby farmers remembered a relative of his, who objected to this rule, painting on his cart-side after his name 'Auctioneer and Valuer, Farmer and Grazier, Publican and Sinner, enough for any silly devil'.
– Beckwith, *Victorian village.*

Description

Dual or multi-occupationists were among the most characteristic talismen of the traditional community, especially the larger communities that could support a wide variety of services, but perhaps not at the level of full-time commitment. The combination of a craft or trade with some part-time farming was such an accepted part of village life that Rose remarked 'no one thought or suggested that cow-keeping and carpentry were other than allied callings'.[1] Collins made much the same point when he stated that 'outside the urban areas a feature of many businesses was diversity and lack of specialisation', going on to report some data from Sun Insurance records of 1821–22 for 110 millers. Second occupations among them included 20 farmers, six each of dealer, gentleman and merchant, four each of brewer, maltster, distiller, baker and paper maker, three factors, two school teachers, one millwright and one workhouse keeper, making a total of 65, or over a half of those recorded.[2]

The well-known writer George Sturt (*alias* Bourne) was brought up in a multi-occupational household. His father was a wheelwright who also had a hop ground, one of many where women, often from London, were employed to do the tying and picking. Moreover, George's mother kept a newsagency and stationery shop at the house where they lived in the small country town of Farnham, Surrey, in the 1860s.[3]

Another instance was an old woman who lived at Aldborough, near Boroughbridge in Yorkshire, before the First World War who remembered that:

> Besides the shop my father had a yeast round, going round all the villages in a seven-mile radius. We also had four fields in which were kept cows, horses, pigs and hens. He also took people to Boroughbridge station in the pony and trap, and the wagonette was used to take our village and local people to whist drives and dances.[4]

Such a man was at the centre of a complex web of relationships and it would be interesting to know how this general factotum described himself to Kelly's agent. However, without the name he might not be recognised, since formal descriptions could vary considerably from reality. Indeed, this is a general

THORPE-ON-THE-HILL.

THORPE-ON-THE-HILL, which has a railway station on the Midland line, between Lincoln and Newark, is a pleasant village, 6 miles S.W. of Lincoln, and has in its parish 350 souls, and 1820 acres of land, belonging to the executors of C. G. Milnes, Esq., and many smaller freeholders. The Dean and Chapter of Lincoln are patrons of the rectory, which is valued in K.B. at £9. 9s. 10¼d., and now at £330, in the incumbency of the Rev. George Frederick Apthorp, B.A., who is Prebendary of Lincoln, where he resides, and who has a farm of 267A. allotted in lieu of tithes, at the enclosure. The Church (All Saints) is a small fabric, with a nave, chancel and tower with two bells. It is heated by means of hot water-pipes laid down in 1868, and contains about 100 sittings. The Wesleyan and the Reform Methodists have each a small chapel here. The poor parishioners have the interest of £40, left by Sir Christopher Nevile and Thomas Sewell. The National School, built in 1843, by the present rector, is attended by about 50 children.

POST OFFICE at Mr. D. Steeper's. Letters arrive at 7.15 a.m., and are despatched at 4.25 p.m., viá Lincoln, which is the nearest Money Order Office.

Alvey Thomas, farmer
Apthorp Rev George Frederick, J.P. rector; h Lincoln
Ashford Joseph, shopkeeper
Bee Thomas, joiner
Brocklesby Benjamin, tailor
Day William, farmer
Dixon Charles, farmer & thrashing machine owner
East Henry, farmer
Eastwood Miss Sarah, National schoolmistress
Foster Henry, farmer; h Sapperton
Fotherby Thomas, farmer, coal merchant and pig jobber
Gibson Miss Rebecca
Gratton James, farmer
Hall Charles, coal merchant and victualler, Railway Hotel

Hansard Robert, shoemaker and shopkeeper
Hunt Thomas, parish clerk
Hunt William, blacksmith
Jackson Jeremiah, farmer and victualler, Sun
Langton John, farmer
Martinson Mrs farmer
Minnitt Hanson, farmer
Newton Goorge, bricklayer
Newton John, farmer
Newton John, jun. farmer and brick & tile manufacturer, Ebenezer hs
Philips James, farm bailiff
Pickwell John, farmer and butcher
Pickwell Matthew, farmer
Pickwell Wm. farmer & cattle dealer
Preston Johnson, shoemaker
Roper William, tailor

Scott John, station master
Sharpe Samuel, farmer and carrier
Skelton Robert, wheelwright
Steeper Drury, postmaster
Stephenson Mrs Mary
Taylor George, farmer
Taylor John, farmer
Taylor William, farmer
Wells William, farmer
Wilmot Mr Benjamin
Wood John, farmer
Woodcock Richard, hawker

RAILWAY STATION on the Midland line. Trains several times a day. John Scott, station master

CARRIER—Saml. Sharpe, to Whisby, Doddington, Skellingthorpe, Boultham and Lincoln, daily

Fig. 5.1. Entry for Thorpe-on-the-Hill, White's *Directory of Lincolnshire*, 1872. Thorpe was an unexceptional example of an English lowland village and parish, but the entry is interesting for its examples of dual occupations (compare with Fig. 4.2) and for the fact that, unusually, the carrier's route to Lincoln was recorded. Perhaps this was because it was so indirect that it was twice as long as the direct route.

problem when dealing with dual occupations in directories, since it is evident from nominal record linkage exercises that a directory entry could leave out as much as it included. Ideally the subject needs to be studied by linking entries for the same person in as many different sources as possible, including the census enumerators' books, parish registers and tithe surveys, to name the most obvious, plus all the directory entries in which the subjects appear. When occupational descriptions occur over several decades the researcher is confronted by the problem that a change of description may record an actual change in occupation, or merely a whim on the part of the subject or the scribe concerned. The most comprehensive view is likely to be gained from account books, but this is a luxury only rarely available (Examples of dual occupations can be seen in Fig. 5.1 and also above, Fig. 4.2 and text re Billinghay and Martin).

Nevertheless, as will be shown presently, directories give a very worthwhile indication of the types of combination in use and their distribution between villages and districts. Hence a few general remarks may be helpful first. It has already been pointed out that the widespread nature of dual occupations in the Victorian period, and their smaller scale survival into the next century, is an indication of the relatively unspecialised nature of the traditional economy. It relates also to the assumption that almost every medieval rural householder, regardless of his main occupation, would have access to some land for the purpose of winning at least a part of his subsistence. Although rapidly declining, such a tradition was still alive a century ago, as in the case of the old woman from Aldborough cited above from *The living village*.

It might be expected, therefore, that the most common combination was that of farming with almost any trade or craft. By the period of directories the farming would usually not be merely for subsistence, but would also represent a smaller scale enterprise of a kind otherwise similar to full-time farms in the same neighbourhood. It is reasonable to assume that many small farms failed to provide a sufficient living for the farm family, which was therefore obliged to find a second occupation to supplement the farm income.

There is also the reverse case to be considered, in which many tradesmen and craftsmen needing their own horse-drawn transport would have a stable on their premises and a paddock at a convenient distance. Such was the arrangement, for example, at the stonemason's house in Low Street, Collingham (Nottinghamshire), with a paddock on Northcroft Lane within five minutes walk. These facilities survived at least into the 1980s, making the house a pleasant residence for anyone with pony-loving children. So the combination of farming with a trade or craft might be one in which the farming was dominant, or merely a minor adjunct hardly to be called farming, or perhaps an even balance between farming and the other occupation.

An important factor in farm work is the fluctuations experienced between the seasons, especially in arable areas where the corn harvest would be a frantic time and a period of winter frost one of relative idleness, during which attention had only to be paid to the farm animals. An alternative occupation might, then, be fitted into the quieter times in the farm calendar. But other occupations also had their seasonal fluctuations, examples being forester, cattle dealer, coal merchant, miller, brick maker, corn merchant, brewer, maltster, lime burner, even the seaside lodging-house keeper. Such men would look for an alternative occupation, as did one of the writer's relatives who combined work in a malt-kiln with a small market garden. Likewise, some industries were afflicted by fluctuations in trade, for example coal mining, many miners having their allotments partly for this reason, partly for subsistence and a breath of fresh air. In a somewhat similar vein some occupations almost by definition had much too small a workload to provide a full week's work: the undertaker, parish clerk, sexton, and some licensees.

In many country districts there was insufficient business to be obtained from a single occupation, owing to lack of population within easy reach, its low purchasing power, and the existence of rivals. These circumstances would encourage men to look for a second occupation to combine with the first. As we have seen, convenient or desirable combinations could include a common use of land by the two occupations, so the farmer might look to cattle-dealing or a butchery business for extra income. A common raw material would draw other occupations together, such as the plumber and the glazier, the miller and the baker, the wheelwright and the joiner or carpenter, the joiner and the undertaker. Finally, the use of transport bought for one purpose might often be put to use for other purposes, as in the Yorkshire case cited above.

Analysis

In previous chapters it has been suggested that multi-occupationists should be counted twice or more times, once under each occupation. This seems to be both the usual and a good practice, since it makes sure that no occupation is left out of the analysis. Whilst a part-time commitment implied a small amount of business, directories, unlike the census enumerators' books, do not provide opportunities to gauge the size of enterprises as measured by the numbers of employees, or by any other means. The accent in studies based on directories is therefore necessarily biased towards the presence or absence of particular services.

The practice of double-counting should, however, be done with care. For example, what is to be made of the following entries in White's *Directory of Lincolnshire* for 1892 under Mareham-le-Fen:

> Chapman, B R & Son, grocers, drapers, clothiers, outfitters, corn, flour and cake merchants, drysalters and dealers in paper-hangings.
> Chapman, Benjamin Ranshaw (and Son), postmaster.

The fact that cake merchants were selling cattle cake to farmers (and were not confectioners!) alerts the reader to at least two different types of trade. The retail trade of groceries, draperies and other items addressed the populace at large and might be covered by the omnibus term 'shopkeeper'. The wholesale supplies to farmers could all be subsumed under 'farmers' merchant'. Such a procedure could reduce to three the number of times Ranshaws are counted : 'shopkeeper, postmaster, and farmers' merchant'. (Drysalters cured meat and other foods by drying and salting). Whatever the decision in this particular instance, the aim should be for consistency in counting (see also Chapter 2).

The same should be said about the definition of certain occupations that were so commonly combined that they were in effect a single occupation. One of the most consistent combinations is 'plumber and glazier'. Since the common denominator down to the introduction of wooden window frames around 1700 was working with lead, it is reasonable to regard these two occupations as one. They stayed together until the late nineteenth century. Cross reference to other sources, including other directories, often reveals the omission of a reference to glazing work. Thus 'plumber' on its own probably embraced the work of the glazier. (In the Victorian period plumbing as now known was in its infancy and most lead work other than 'leaded lights' involved guttering and the sealing of roofs, or in some cases the roofs themselves). Other common combinations that might be regarded as one occupation for counting purposes include: chemist and druggist, builder and bricklayer, wine and spirit merchant, watch and clockmaker, boot and shoemaker, farmer and grazier, tailor and draper, saddler and harness maker.

Table 5.1a   East Lincolnshire analysis of dual occupations: excluded combinations

Baker and flour dealer	Grocer and draper (because of ambiguity in White's presentation)
Blacksmith and machine maker	Joiner and builder
Boot and shoemaker	Nurseryman and seedsman
Brewer and maltster	Plumber and glazier
Brickmaker and tilemaker	Rope and sacking manufacturer
Bricklayer and mason	Rope and twine manufacturer
Bricklayer and builder	Saddler and harness maker
Carpenter, joiner and wheelwright	Seed and cake merchant (= farmer's merchant)
Chemist and druggist	Tailor and draper
Draper and dressmaker	Tinner and brazier
Farmer and grazier	Watch and clockmaker
Fisherman and oyster dealer	Wine and spirit merchant

Source: White's *Directory of Lincolnshire*, 1856. Tables 5.1a–5.4 are based on data for the following areas: the sokes of Bolingbroke and Horncastle, and the wapentakes of Gartree, Walshcroft, Kirton (Holland) and Bradley Haverstoe, containing 145 villages and a population of 60,000 in 1851 (pp. 472-91, 552-572, and 733-819).

The full list of such excluded combinations used in a study in east Lincolnshire can be seen in Table 5.1a. Other exclusions are listed in Table 5.1b, and are of two types. First, there is a set of synonyms accepted for the exercise, for example, corn dealer was taken as the same as corn merchant, thus having the effect of excluding corn dealer as a separate occupation. (However, one is less certain that a wood dealer was carrying on the same trade as the timber merchant, as the first might refer to firewood and rough timber and the second to sawn timber). Secondly, some occupations appear to have consumed so little time that they can hardly rank even as 'part-time', for example, the sexton who, in some small parishes, only sprang into activity once or twice a year.

The east Lincolnshire study is not meant to set up an authoritative standard, since it is based on only one directory and, although taking in 145 villages, it is confined to a single county. Different results might be expected even in the same area if a different directory were used, especially if brought out by a different publisher. For example, the author was obliged to regard 'grocer and draper' as an excluded combination because the lay-out of White's entries made it impossible to distinguish consistently between men who were one or the other or both. Nevertheless, the results as seen in Tables 5.2–5.4 give a broad idea of what to expect and provide a point of comparison with studies elsewhere.

Table 5.1b   East Lincolnshire analysis of dual occupations: other exclusions

Synonyms	Minor part-time occupations
Agent, dealer and merchant, when accompanied by similar adjectives, e.g., corn dealer = corn merchant	Bathing machine owners: large number in Cleethorpes, even in 1856 a seaside resort
Similarly wood dealer = timber merchant	Insurance agent
Innkeeper, tavern and victualler	Landowner
Land agent, estate steward	Parish clerk
Patent medicine dealer = chemist	Post office: functions at this date were only spasmodically reported by White.
Machine maker and machinist	Registrar
	Sexton

Source: As for Table 5.1a.

The total number of men with multi-occupations identified in the exercise area was 202. Some followed more than two occupations, and hence there were 221 different combinations. Altogether 37 different occupations occurred as the first-cited occupation in a combination, and 52 occupations, many of them the same, occurred as second-cited occupations. Such a wide spread of different occupations meant that the most common combinations (Table 5.2) did not account for a very large proportion of the total number of multi-occupationists, miller-baker and baker-miller combinations being the only two to score in double figures.

Table 5.3 shows a very wide difference in the number of occasions upon which even the most commonly recurring occupations were to be found in multi-occupational combinations. In first place were the millers with a count of 44, in second place their frequent 'partners' the bakers with 42, but in 16th place the carriers appeared only eight times. Following them was the long string of other occupations mentioned in the previous paragraph. Comparison with the tables in Chapter 6 shows that about half of the commonly combined occupations were, as one would expect, among the occupations with the largest number of members; but several occupations in Table 5.3 are among the less well-represented occupations, carrier, corn merchant and cattle dealer among them.

The leading occupations appear again in Table 5.4 in an analysis showing that some were combined with a much narrower choice of second occupations than others. Thus, despite their high scores in Table 5.3, the millers and bakers combined with very few other occupations, whereas the less common calling of coal merchant was combined with no less than 11 other occupations when it was cited first, and five more when cited second. The two entries for farmers are especially instructive, since farmer comes out overwhelmingly as a first-cited occupation. Presumably many of the trades/craftsmen who occupied small amounts of land for one or more of the reasons noticed above did not think of themselves as farmers. In their minds, and probably objectively too, the land was only an adjunct to their main activity.

Table 5.2   **East Lincolnshire: six most common combinations of occupations**

Combination	Number of cases
Miller-baker	18
Baker-miller	13
Farmer-cattle dealer	9
Brewer and/or maltster-victualler	6
Farmer-miller	5
Coal merchant-corn merchant	4

Source: As for Table 5.1a

Table 5.3   **East Lincolnshire: 16 most common occupations involved in multi-occupational combinations**

Occupation	Number of cases
Miller	44
Baker	42
Shopkeeper	34
Grocer/draper	32
Farmer	30
Victualler	29
Beerhouse keeper	22
Coal merchant	22
Carpenter/joiner/wheel-wright	17
Brewer/maltster	16
Butcher	14
Cattle dealer	13
Blacksmith/smith	12
Corn merchant	10
Boot/shoemaker	8
Carrier	8

Source: As for Table 5.1a.

Table 5.4 East Lincolnshire: analysis of combinations of leading occupations

Occupation	Cited first/second	No. of other occupations, with which combined	Total
Farmer	1	10	
Farmer	2	1	11
Grocer/draper	1	18	
Grocer/draper	2	4	22
Baker	1	3	
Baker	2	5	8
Shopkeeper	1	12	
Shopkeeper	2	9	21
Miller	1	3	
Miller	2	5	8
Coal merchant	1	11	
Coal merchant	2	5	16
Beerhouse keeper	1	8	
Beerhouse keeper	2	7	15
Carpenter/joiner/wheelwright	1	10	
Carpenter etc	2	3	13

Source: As for Table 5.1a.

Evidence from the censuses

This is a point on which the directories appear to be sharply different from the census enumerators' books, which include a large number of men who followed householders' instructions carefully and recorded the farming of land as well as a trade or craft. In the census report of 1851, 22,982 dual occupationists appear in Table LXXXVII which lists the hundreds of different 'pursuits beside farming' in which they were engaged.

Table 5.5 contains the 18 most common of these pursuits, all followed by more than 300 persons, with farming as an additional interest. At the top of the list are 1,898 persons described as licensed victuallers and/or beerhouse keepers, the 1,885 millers coming a very close second. However, to represent the drink trade as a whole it is necessary to add in the innkeepers and maltsters, a total of 3,971 being the result, outnumbering the millers by a ratio of two to one. Both kinds of combination made good sense. The miller had corn of his own to process if he was also a farmer, whilst conversely the addition of value to

Table 5.5 Occupiers of land engaged in other pursuits beside farming, 1851, England and Wales - the 18 most common pursuits

Pursuit	Number	Pursuit	Number
Victualler and/or beerhouse	1898	Blacksmith	645
Miller	1885	Woollen cloth manufacturer	631
Innkeeper	1536	Shoemaker	546
Gardener, nurseryman	1463	Carman, carrier	543
Butcher	1352	Maltster	537
Land proprietor	1230	Mason, pavior	445
Farm bailiff	895	Coal miner	315
Carpenter, joiner	759	Cotton manufacturer	315
Grocer	690	House proprietor	313

Source: *Census of Great Britain 1851*, BPP 1852-3, LXXXVIII, Pt 1, being Population Tables II, vol I, page cclxxxv, Table XXXVII. This table excludes many other dual occupationists (but an unknown number) who were transferred to farmer tables because they reported the sizes of their holdings and the numbers of labourers employed (for background see Mills, 'Farm statistics').

his product was an incentive for a farmer. Those who kept hostelries providing changes of horses and accommodation for visitors' horses found the occupation of land a necessity. As the smaller licensed premises did not represent a full-time occupation, spare time could be spent on the land.

As to be expected, Table 5.5 includes several more common occupations, but there are others demanding comment. Approximately 1,500 persons recorded investment in land or house property, which was hardly an occupation in the conventional sense, and there must have been many more in this position who did not think to report it on their census schedules. About the same number combined farming with market gardens and plant nurseries and may again be only a fraction of those so engaged: for example, think of the large number of fruit farms in Kent and the large acreages of cider apples in the West Country. Nearly 900 farm bailiffs were managing another man's farm at the same time as farming on their own account, probably on a much smaller scale. About 300 miners may have concentrated their farming activities into the slacker days of the summer half of the year, when the demand for house coal would be low. Finally, there were some 950 cotton or woollen cloth manufacturers who were also significant occupiers of land. This combination seems strange at first sight, but in 1851 the practice of 'tentering' out cloth to dry and bleach was presumably still in use, and this would have been facilitated by manufacturers engaging seriously in farming.

This chapter has acted as a preliminary stage in the analysis of directory material relating to trades and crafts serving the countryside. The main analysis now follows, divided into three stages each represented in a separate chapter. The first stage concentrates on the self-sufficiency of the traditional village, a notion often asserted, but less often supported by a serious weight of evidence. The second stage demonstrates that interdependence between villages was a common feature of rural life, since there were many villages too small for self-sufficiency, no matter how this is defined. The third stage shows how the countryside relied upon towns for services of a higher order, or simply for greater choice. Thus relationships both within and between communities are exemplified.

NOTES

1. Rose, *Village carpenter*, 12.
2. Collins, 'Introduction to Chapter 5', 393.
3. Sturt, *A small boy*, 2, 70–71, and 98.
4. Jennings, *Living village*, 78.

CHAPTER SIX

VILLAGE SELF-SUFFICIENCY IN DECLINE

The old independence of the countryside and its near self-sufficiency was whittled away by the growth of town-based dealers who brought round their factory-made bread and clothing, their branded groceries and railway-carried fish. Town emporiums drove the village craftsmen out of business, unless they could survive by turning to some new specialisation. The professional men, too, who had once been quite numerous in the larger villages, were not replaced as they moved out or retired.   – Mingay, *The Victorian countryside*, vol 1, 8.

The decline in the rural population from about the third quarter of last century and the effects of the railways bringing in factory-made goods form the background against which the rural economy gradually weakened. But what did it weaken from? Just how independent of the towns were the supposedly self-sufficient villages? One recent definition of basic self-sufficiency, grounded in a study of 31 north Hertfordshire villages, is that to qualify as self-sufficient a village should have had at least one blacksmith, a carpenter or wheelwright, and a boot and shoemaker representing essential crafts; and at least one grocer or general shopkeeper and one licensed premises, representing the essential retailers.[1] This definition will be used here as a starting point for an enquiry into the kinds of services we can expect to find recorded in a typical village about 1850, when the rural economy was perhaps at its strongest.

Thornborough, Bucks: the experience of one village

The first stratagem in the enquiry is the analysis of data for one village: Thornborough, Buckinghamshire. With a peak population of 762, Thornborough was among the larger villages of north Buckinghamshire: seven times the size of its neighbour and near namesake Thornton, but somewhat smaller than some other neighbours, such as Great Horwood and Padbury, and only a quarter of the size of Buckingham, the nearest market town three miles away (Figs. 6.1–6.2; see Fig 7.2 for location map).

Thornborough experienced much the same changes in population as rural England as a whole, but with some local variations. There was a sharper increase in the early nineteenth century: 66 per cent higher at the 1841 peak than in 1801, compared with the national rural increase of 40 per cent. This peak was 20 years earlier than the overall rural peak, perhaps because grassland farming and lacemaking could not sustain the increases of earlier years. Population sank steadily from 1841 to 1931, when it reached 420, a point lower than it had been in 1801. The 1931 situation can be explained partly in terms of Thornborough's relative isolation from new forms of employment,

THORNBOROUGH CHURCH AND SCHOOLS, NEAR BUCKINGHAM.

WALFORD & SON, PRINTERS, BUCKINGHAM

Figs. 6.1 (upper) and 6.2. Thornborough (Bucks), the village green, c.1910s from post-cards. Directories describe the church as 'a building of stone in the Decorated and Perpendicular styles', and record that it had 300 sittings. In the upper picture, to the right of the church are the two schools, that nearest the church, built in 1840 for 100 children, now being the village hall. The later one with the bell turret, built in 1894 for 120 children, is still in use. To the right of it is the school house of the same date. In the lower picture the panorama continues with the New Inn, long delicensed, a building of the seventeenth century based on a cross-passage design. The thatched cottage behind the men in sunhats is still thatched, but no longer a shop.

Table 6.1 Summary of enterprises and services at Thornborough, Bucks, 1848-1985

Date	Types of services	Total enterprises	Dual occupationists
1848	13	24	7
1853	18	39	10
1864	15	26	7
1865	14	23	5
1883	14	24	5
1891	13	22	3
1907	12	18	Nil
1915	9	13	1
1928	9	12	1
1939	7	8	1
1985	6	7	Nil

Sources: *Directories of Buckinghamshire* published by Kelly, except for 1853 (Craven and Musson), 1865 (Cassey) and 1985 (local knowledge).

despite being only 55 miles from London. Long-distance commuting by car and rail did not begin in this area until after the Second World War. Buckingham was in a declining state for most of the period, providing relatively little employment for local villages. The 1960s, however, saw the influx of commuters, and by 1981 the population stood at 553.

Thornborough possessed all of Crompton's basic services and more besides throughout the period before the First World War. The figures in Table 6.1 summarise the numbers of *types* of services offered: for the most part these were commercial services, but the school and the police constable have been added, and other social services (such as doctor or nurse) would have been added too if they had existed there. The range of services was at its greatest in 1853: this might be a real peak, but the total of 18 might merely represent the greater care of Craven and Musson's man, compared with the men from Kelly's. Putting the 1853 figures on one side, the range remained steady at 12-15 services from 1848 until 1907. The First World War appears to be the watershed, with a decline down to seven in 1939.

Although the maximum number of services offered at any one time was 18 in 1853, altogether 24 different types of service are recorded in the directories, as various services came and went. Services that disappeared never to return include those shown in Table 6.2. Early to go was the last tailor, a common experience elsewhere, but the decline seen in this way is as gradual as shown in Table 6.1. Unlike many other villages, Thornborough did not attract any of

Table 6.2 Periods during which services disappeared from Thornborough

Tailor	1853–1865	Brickmaker	1891–1907	Butcher	1915–28
Maltster	1865–1883	Wheelwright	1891–1907	Carrier	1928–39
Shoemaker	1883–1891	Blacksmith	1915–1928	Baker	After 1939
				Corn-miller	After 1939

Sources: As for Table 5.1.

the new types of service in the earlier part of the twentieth century, except that the carrier was partly replaced by the outside company that started a bus service. There was no garage, no agricultural engineer, no fish-and-chip shop, no ladies' hairdresser and probably no one charging accumulators for wireless sets.

Another measure of decline in the rural economy is the process by which many services represented by several enterprises in the mid-nineteenth century might run down to a single enterprise each before disappearing altogether. At Thornborough this applied to the public houses of which there were once five, but only two in 1985, when the pub was the only type of service with more than one outlet. There were four enterprises in 1848 described as carpenter, joiner or wheelwright, descriptions overlapping so much that they must be counted together. There were once four shopkeepers/ grocers, three each of bricklayers, shoemakers, bakers, milliners, and stonemasons, and two each of carriers, blacksmiths, maltsters, butchers and sawyers. Hidden from view by the directories are figures for the whole workforce engaged in trades and crafts, since journeymen, assistants and apprentices were only recorded in the census enumerators' books. However, since many rural craftsmen worked on their own or with only one helper, the directories are not as seriously defective in rural areas, in this respect, as they are in towns, where enterprises tended to be much larger. A significant number of enterprises were, indeed, run by dual occupationists: small farms acted as a base in eight cases at Thornborough among the peak number of ten dual-occupationists recorded in 1853 by the careful Craven and Musson.

The general view

It would be dangerous to rely on one village for a general view of the subject. Some help can be obtained from Wrigley's study of 'Men on the land and men in the countryside', an article that makes an interesting distinction between the slow growth of agricultural employment and the much more rapid growth of traditional rural crafts and trades in the first half of the nineteenth century. This was mainly due to the increasing prosperity of the countryside. Even in the 17 most rural counties the number of men engaged in ten major retail and handicraft employments rose from about 134,000 in 1831 to about 164,000 in 1851, enough to raise their proportion of the workforce from 17.2 to 18.1 per cent.[2]

Chartres looked at occupational census figures over the same period in a different way, but arrived at similar conclusions and in particular drew attention to the disproportionate growth at the national level in the numbers of men employed in transport services. Thus the number of carriers rose from 12,800 in 1831 to 44,000 in 1851, partly because of the need for feeder services to the new railway stations. Similarly, there was a rapid increase in the numbers of farriers and blacksmiths from 52,000 to 100,000, wheelwrights from 18,000 to 28,000 and saddlers and harness makers from 6,000 to 15,000.[3] This analysis relates to the whole country, but as England and Wales did not become half-urban until a point in the 1840s, it is reasonable to assume that these rapid increases were shared by rural areas in a significant measure. After the mid-century, when the rural population began to stagnate and then to fall, there was probably a slowing down in the expansion, followed by a decline.

This decline has not yet been analysed from census figures for the whole of rural England, but two sets of figures have been produced for crafts in areas of significant size: Rutland and the South Hams district of Devon, both of which included a few small towns. Using directories, the numbers of rural craft enterprises in the 18 parishes of South Hams fell from 238 in 1850 to 61 in 1939. The 1939 figure is only a quarter of the 1850 figure, whereas population over the same period fell only to about three-quarters of the 1851 level. Similarly, in Rutland the numbers of rural craftsmen (excluding the building trades) enumerated in the censuses fell from 810 in 1851 to 190 in 1931, the latter figure being a little under a quarter of the earlier figure, much the same trend as in South Hams. Building trades in Rutland had held up much better, as their numbers in 1931 were at 60 per cent of the 1851 level, whereas in South Hams their numbers had gone down in step with those of other crafts. The total population of Rutland fell: in 1931 it was about 80 per cent of the 1851 level — quite close to the trend in South Hams.[4] The decline of rural crafts was therefore far steeper than the decline in rural population, a not surprising conclusion, since these crafts were rapidly becoming obsolete.

The relative importance of different trades and crafts in 1851 can be seen in Table 6.3. Exact comparisons will, however, not be possible with data derived from directory entries for rural communities, since the table is based on census data, which include all workmen, and the figures are biased by the inclusion of towns with villages. There is also the problem of terminology: do carpenters include joiners, do shopkeepers include grocers and drapers? But the table provides a starting point for determining a local list of trades and crafts that can be regarded as essential for village self-sufficiency. Notice the wide disparity between the top and bottom of the table: there were four times as many shoemakers in rural counties as bakers and butchers. This might be taken as a reflection of the relative independence of households in food provision, and the relatively small amount of capital with which it was possible to enter the shoemaking, carpentry and tailoring trades.

Comparison with Crompton's list of five basic services is instructive. These appear in the first seven positions in the 'rural counties' column in Table 6.3, but tailoring and the building trades come above the publican, who is in the

Table 6.3 Employment in 10 leading trades and crafts, 1851, males aged 20 and over

1,000s	Rural Counties	Rank order	1,000s	England	Rank order
34.5	Shoemaker	1	153.3	Shoemaker	1
29.7	Carpenter	2	116.1	Carpenter	2
17.4	Tailor	3	86.0	Tailor	3
16.4	Blacksmith	4	66.6	Blacksmith	4
15.1	Mason	5	60.1	Shopkeeper	5
11.4	Shopkeeper	6	56.3	Mason	6
11.4	Publican	7	54.6	Bricklayer	7
10.1	Bricklayer	8	48.2	Publican	8
9.7	Butcher	9	44.7	Butcher	9
8.6	Baker	10	34.3	Baker	10

Note: The 'rural' counties were taken as Bedfordshire, Berkshire, Buckinghamshire, Cambridgeshire, Cumberland, Devon, Dorset, Herefordshire, Huntingdonshire, Lincolnshire, Norfolk, Oxfordshire, Rutland, Somerset, Suffolk, Westmorland and Wiltshire.

Source: Wrigley, 'Men on the land', 300-01, based on the 1851 Census.

lowest position occupied by any of her chosen services. Nevertheless, the congruence is relatively good, bearing in mind the different ways in which the two lists were derived. It could be argued that the services of a mason or a bricklayer (depending on the district) would be needed much less often than any of Crompton's list, and the relatively large numbers so employed probably reflect in part the needs of growing towns in even the 'rural counties' as defined by Wrigley. Tailoring is a different matter: its appearance in the third rank in this table suggests that it could be regarded as a basic craft in 1851, but soon to be overtaken by the drapery selling ready-made clothing.

Some intermediate case studies

How much difference was there between villages of different sizes? An example from Leicestershire is derived from White's *Directory of Leicestershire* for 1863. On the marlstone hills between Melton Mowbray and Belvoir Castle are the villages of Scalford, which had a population of 553 in 1861, Goadby Marwood 195, and the hamlets of Wycomb and Chadwell forming one township, which could only muster 139 people between them. In 1863, the sole tradesman in Wycomb and Chadwell was Spencer Marshall, grocer and draper. At Goadby services were considerably better, encouraged perhaps by having its meagre population in a single nucleus: in addition to a general shop, there was a carpenter, shoemaker, stonemason, tailor and a thrashing machine proprietor. Scalford possessed all of these except the latter and also had at least one each of baker, blacksmith, butcher, cattle dealer, carrier, maltster, miller, publican, schoolmaster and wheelwright, 15 services

Table 6.4 Populations of 20 north-east Leicestershire villages, 1861 and 1911

Village	1861	1911	Village	1861	1911
Nether Broughton	481	380	Knipton	369	280
Long Clawson	820	735	Branston	297	222
Hose	477	411	Eaton	422	436
Harby	655	603	Eastwell	160	194
Stathern	524	578	Goadby Marwood	195	176
Plungar	251	184	Wycomb & Chadwell	139	103
Barkestone	411	253	Scalford	553	688
Redmile	521	382	Holwell	147	249
Belvoir	171	111	Ab Kettleby	224	267
Harston	164	157	Wartnaby	116	89

Sources: as for Table 6.5.

altogether. The point is easily made that small villages, of which there were thousands, might be far removed from a state of self-sufficiency, no matter how defined.

With the help of a suitable directory, it is possible to do some simple calculations to find out which were the most widespread services, and how large on average villages needed to be to provide a living for different kinds of trade or craft enterprises. The 20 north-east Leicestershire villages in Table 6.4 had populations spread out fairly evenly from 116 to 820 in 1861 and from 89 to 735 in 1911. Table 6.5 shows the results of the simplest and quickest type of calculations, indicating how common it was in relative terms for particular services to be offered in this group of villages. The combined category of grocer and shopkeeper was present in 17 out of the 20 villages in 1863 and in 16 in 1911, and therefore ranked first. At the bottom of the rank order in 1863 were the saddlers, who were present in only four villages, whilst in 1911 the bottom position was occupied by the corn millers. Some occupations have been combined as either synonymous or overlapping in such a way that consistent distinctions are impossible: for example, bricklayers, masons and builders. Experience in different parts of the country might suggest different combinations, as some terms were more commonly used in some areas than others, or were used in different ways.

When the same procedure is repeated at two different dates there is an opportunity to observe not only the rise or fall in the overall provision of services but, through the changes in rank order, also the varying experiences of different trades and crafts. Thus in north-east Leicestershire there was an overall decline in services and there were, for example, only 10 villages with bakers in 1911, compared with 12 in 1863. But bakers had become more

Table 6.5   Presence/absence of 11 selected trade and craft enterprises in 20 north-east Leicestershire villages

Trade/craft	1863 Number	1863 Rank	1911 Number	1911 Rank
Baker	12	6.5=	10	4
Blacksmith	12	6.5=	9	5
Boot and shoemaker	15	3=	5	8.5=
Bricklayer/ mason/builder	10	8	6	7
Butcher	9	9.5=	8	6
Corn miller	9	9.5=	3	11
Grocer/shopkeeper	17	1	16	1
Joiner/carpenter/wh'lwright	15	3=	12	3
Public house/inn	15	3=	14	2
Saddler/harnessmaker	4	11	5	8.5=
Tailor	14	5	4	10

Note: See Table 6.4 for names of the villages.

Sources: White's *Directory of Leicestershire*, 1863 and Kelly's *Directory of Leicestershire*, 1916.

important, having moved up in rank order from 6.5 to 3, presumably as home-baking declined. Butchers also improved their position, as reliance on home-killed animals declined, and prosperity possibly increased among the labourers. A steep decline among the shoemakers and tailors can be noted; and two-thirds of the villages possessing a corn mill in 1863 had lost it by 1911.

Table 6.6 represents an attempt to answer the question as to what village population levels, or thresholds, were required to sustain a particular service in 1863. This threshold is defined as the midpoint between the average population of villages *having* a particular service and the average population of villages *not having* that service (see Appendix 6.1 for a guide to calculation). For example, 12 villages with an average population of 480 contained at least one baker, whilst the eight bakerless villages not surprisingly had the much smaller average population of only 168. The midpoint between 168 and 480 is 324, the population taken as the approximate minimum number of people needed in one village to provide a sufficient market for a single baker to become established there.

A comparison between Tables 6.5 and 6.6 shows generally similar rank order positions, confirming the broad reliability of the two different methods of calculation in relation to the relative importance of different services. Thus, in both cases the grocer/shopkeeper was the most important service, that is, the

Table 6.6   Threshold levels by population in 20 north-east Leicestershire and 31 north Hertfordshire villages, 1863 and 1850

Trade/craft	Leics 1863 Population	Leics 1863 Rank	Herts 1850 Population	Herts 1850 Rank
Baker	324	6	829	9
Blacksmith	328	7	753	4.5=
Boot and shoemaker	311	5	753	4.5=
Bricklayer/ mason/builder	355	8.5=	878	10
Butcher	355	8.5=	794	6
Corn miller	369	10	813	7
Grocer/shopkeeper	274	1	606	2
Joiner/carpenter/wh'lwright	307	4	707	3
Public house/inn	291	2	547	1
Saddler/harnessmaker	422	11	949	11
Tailor	297	3	822	8

Sources: For Leicestershire: White's *Directory of Leicestershire*, 1863 and Kelly's *Directory of Leicestershire*, 1916. For Hertfordshire: Crompton, 'Changes in rural service occupations', 199.

most commonly encountered service, and the saddler was the least common. There were, of course, many even less common services that have not been included in the tables, such as the general practitioner at Long Clawson, the plumber and glazier at Harby, and the carriers in many villages. Choosing a group of services to represent self-sufficiency is bound in some measure to be arbitrary.

Table 6.6 also affords a comparison between villages in two different counties, in which the rank order positions of the services are reassuringly similar. The only really wide divergence is in the positions of the tailors, who were much more common in north-east Leicestershire than in Hertfordshire villages in the Stevenage and Buntingford areas.[5] It is tempting to suggest that Leicestershire people, living in the 'high' wage area of the Midlands and the north, were better able to afford tailor-made clothes in preference to ready-to-wear items from factories.

Such an argument might be more powerful in explaining the marked contrast in actual threshold levels between the two areas, since in Hertfordshire a village had to be more than twice as big as in Leicestershire in order to provide a market for a particular service. For example, the threshold for grocer/shopkeeper in north Hertfordshire was 606, but only 274 in north-east Leicestershire. However, there may be other factors to consider, such as the sizes of enterprises, the distances between villages, the way in which the population was distributed between different townships, whether it was concentrated in villages or scattered between hamlets and outlying farms, and so on.

A further comparison of thresholds is made possible by Table 6.7, but only at a broad level. Whereas the dates and methods of classification and calculation are similar for the Hertfordshire and Leicestershire villages, the basis of comparison with the North Riding and Norfolk is less robust, with widely differing dates and selections of services in use. Nevertheless, there is general agreement that basic services should include a food shop, a pub or inn, a wheelwright or carpenter, with the blacksmith a little further behind. The saddler and harness-maker is seen as one of the most specialist craftsmen in the list. Indeed, it is known that he would often go out to farms at a distance from his workshop, staying there for several days until all the harness had been repaired. This is a good illustration of the way in which the market areas of trades/craftsmen were extended beyond the confines of their own villages, and points to the fact that the figures of threshold populations do not include the whole of these markets.

Finally, threshold levels may have varied over time, going up as crafts declined and enough customers could only be found in larger villages and over wider areas. Thus threshold levels for shoemakers went up in Wensleydale between 1841 and 1881, but declined in Swaledale.[6] In northeast Leicestershire they were much the same in 1916 as they had been in 1863, whilst even more surprisingly they went down consistently, except for tailors, between 1850 and 1890 in the north Hertfordshire villages.[7] Clearly there is scope for much more research on this aspect of the subject.

This chapter has shown that village self-sufficiency in services was far more widespread in the nineteenth than in the twentieth century. Each household could place considerable reliance on other households in the same village, and relationships between them must have been all the richer for that reason, among others, than they were to become in later periods. However, there was considerable variation between communities of different sizes: in particular the minority of the population living in small villages, often without a full set of Crompton's basic list of services, had to depend on bigger villages nearby, or on town outlets. Moreover, the rate at which services declined varied considerably from one service and one district to another, but in general the decline was probably slower than has often been implied. Perhaps the First World War was the great watershed. The study of Swaledale and Wensleydale, for example, confirms Saville's conclusion that whilst decline occurred in the late nineteenth century, many crafts survived into the twentieth.[8]

Table 6.7 Comparison of threshold levels by rank order in four areas

Rank	Leicestershire 1863	Hertfordshire 1850	Norfolk 1836	North Riding 1879
1	Grocer/shopkeeper	Public house/inn	Publican	Publican
2	Public house/inn	Grocer/shopkeeper	Shopkeeper	Shopkeeper
3	Tailor	Joiner/carp/wheel't	Blacksmith	Tailor
4	Joiner/carp/wheel't	Blacksmith, 4.5=	Grocer	Blacksmith
5	Boot/shoemaker	Boot /shoemaker, 4.5=	Wheelwright	Wheelwright
6	Baker	Butcher	Saddler	Butcher
7	Blacksmith	Miller		Mason
8	Bricklayer etc, 8.5=	Tailor		Grocer
9	Butcher, 8.5=	Baker		Saddler
10	Miller	Bricklayer etc		
11	Saddler	Saddler		

Sources For Leicestershire and Hertfordshire - as for Table 5.6; for Norfolk and the North Riding of Yorkshire - Chartres, 'Country tradesmen', 304 and Chartres and Turnbull, 'Country craftsmen', 321.

Appendix 6.1: Guide to calculation of threshold levels

For comparative purposes, the calculations of threshold levels in this chapter have followed the practice of Chartres. He defined the threshold level of population for a service as the midpoint between the average (mean) population of villages having that service and those without the service. Taking the example of bakers in the Leicestershire villages used for Table 4.6, the 12 villages with bakers had populations as follows: 481, 820, 477, 655, 524, 411, 521, 369, 297, 422, 553, and 224. These sum to 5,724, which when divided by 12 gives a mean of 479.5 persons per village. The eight bakerless villages had populations of 251, 171, 164, 160, 195, 139, 147, and 116, summing to 1,343, or a mean of 167.8 persons. Rounding to the nearest whole number, the threshold = the midpoint between 168 and 480

$$= 168 + \frac{480-168}{2}$$

$$= 168 + 156$$

$$= 324 \text{ persons.}$$

Those with a little more statistical inclination might use medians instead of means in this calculation, since this guards against erratic results arising from skew in the data. In the example above it makes little difference, since the midpoint would have been 162 + 479-162/2; = 162 + 317/2; = 162 + 158.5; = 320.5, or rounded to 321 persons.

NOTES

1. Crompton, *Self-sufficiency*, especially 136–38.
2. Wrigley, 'Men on the land', 300.
3. Chartres, 'Trades, crafts and professions', 418.
4. Saville, *Rural depopulation*, 74, 76, 174–85, and 212.
5. Crompton, 'Changes in rural service occupations', 195 and 199.
6. Hallas, 'Craft occupations', 26.
7. Crompton, 'Changes in rural service occupations', 199.
8. Hallas, 'Craft occupations', 27–28.
9. Chartres, 'Country craftsmen', 304 and Chartres and Turnbull, 'Country tradesmen', 321. Their threshold levels refer to Norfolk (1836) and the North Riding of Yorkshire (1879).

CHAPTER SEVEN

VILLAGE INTERDEPENDENCE

...while butcher-less Naseby seeks meat from Clipston, villagers from the latter can avail themselves of Naseby's garage and service-station facilities which they themselves lack...   - Weekley, 'Lateral interdependence', 369.

Assumptions

As the above quotation from Weekley makes clear, it would be wrong to think of villages as islands somehow unconnected to each other and it is not difficult to think of other present-day instances of country people travelling between villages for particular services. For example, a cross-country journey to the vet, from Thornborough to Padbury, or to Maids Moreton, was a familiar experience when the author lived in Thornborough. Naturally we went by car, which liberated us from using bus routes centred on Buckingham (Fig. 7.2). But in the days when there was neither bus, nor car, nor bicycle, people thought nothing of walking a few miles, often by more direct paths now disused. Moreover, as today, a good many services came into the village in some portable form: the chapman and pedlar with their sacks over their shoulders; the doctor on his rounds with pony and trap; the miller's wagon collecting corn for grinding and delivering the resulting flour; or the Aldborough (Yorkshire) shopkeeper with his yeast round mentioned in Chapter 5.

In the period after the First World War it was possible for village suppliers to extend the range of their deliveries by using motor vans. One especially large rural bakery is remembered at Branston (Lincolnshire), where William Young had a fleet of eight vans, all 'Rattling Tin-Lizzies' (Fords). Edward Lintin the butcher operated in a similar way, sending his delivery men out to customers up to ten miles away. Many of these lived in isolated fen and heathland farms and cottages, sometimes as much as four or five miles away from the nearest village. Idyllic in fine weather, the roads proved to be lonely places when it came to digging a van out of a snow-drift!

This chapter concentrates on relationships *between* communities, as they can be inferred from directory entries. Occasionally a tradesman's account book can be found containing the addresses of his customers, and this is the surest way of identifying the territory he covered (see Chapter 9). Newspaper advertisements might also indicate the area in which a tradesman offered a service (Fig 7.1). However, the directories, with their wealth of information, can be made to throw some light on the interdependence which existed between neighbouring villages, provided that a few qualifications are kept in mind.

THE GREAT NORTHERN COAL DEPOTS,

BOURNE AND NAVENBY.

E. CHAMBERLAIN,

COAL, COKE & GENERAL MERCHANT,

TAKES this opportunity of calling the particular attention of the Inhabitants of Bourne, Navenby, Bassingham, Aubourne, and adjoining Villages, to the great advantage they will derive from purchasing COAL at either of the above Stations, where the best Coals only are kept, and offered at the lowest possible price.

Every description of CAKE, CORN, SALT, MANURE, &c., supplied at the shortest notice.

E. C. has made arrangements for the SOLE AGENCY of the Celebrated DOG KENNELS LIME, at all Stations between LINCOLN and PETERBOROUGH, and begs to call attention to the following:—

Price of LIME per Ton, delivered carriage free, at the following Stations :—Lincoln, 13s.; Waddington, 13s. 4d.; Navenby, 13s. 8d.; Leadenham, 14s.; Caythorpe, 14s. 3d.; Honington, 14s. 6d.; Grantham, 14s. 4d.; Sleaford, 14s. 8d.; Ancaster, 14s. 8d.; Heckington, 14s. 8d.; Swineshead, 15s.; Hubbert's Bridge, 15s. 2d.; Boston, 14s. 8d.; Spalding, 15s. 4d.; Holbeach, 15s. 9d.; Long Sutton, 17s.; St. James Deeping, 15s. 6d.; Peterborough, 15s. 2d.; Bourne, 15s. 4d.

TERMS :—CASH MONTHLY.

Agent for the Church of England Life and Fire Assurance Trust and Annuity Institution, 9 & 10, King street, Cheapside, London. All letters, &c., to be addressed Bourne, Lincolnshire.

Fig 7.1 Advertisement from White's *Directory of Lincolnshire*, 1872. Not many village enterprises could afford advertisements in directories, and relied instead on word of mouth, and the local newspapers and parish magazines. This advertisement was inserted by a firm with its main location in a market town (Bourne) and a village branch at Navenby and from the latter depot it supplied several adjoining villages. Chamberlain concentrated on the transport of heavy materials to country areas, but he was also agent for an insurance company.

As we have already seen, directory descriptions do not necessarily indicate the full range of services offered: a joiner might do some wheelwrighting; a grocer might have a small drapery section not mentioned, and so on.

Whilst we can find the nearest village with a particular service, we cannot be sure that was the point to which people resorted automatically. They may have preferred to walk twice as far in order to visit the shop or workshop of their choice. By the same token, they may have gone outside their own village, even when one of its own inhabitants offered the service required.

We are unlikely to find information on the transport facilities at the disposal of tradesmen. For instance, not every miller would be able to send a wagon to neighbouring villages to collect cottagers' sacks of grain.

In the examples that follow, parishes are treated as points on the map, whereas in fact some of their population lived at outlying farmsteads, like Nash Brakes, on the Nash-Thornborough boundary, or little hamlets, like the Coombes brick-making community on the Thornborough-Padbury boundary.

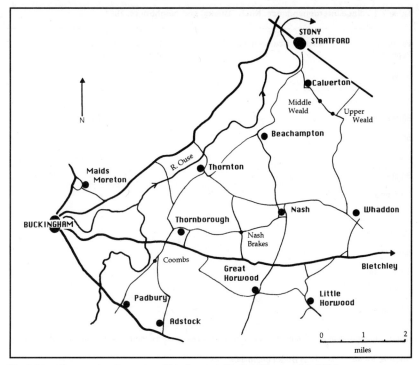

Fig. 7.2 Location map for villages near Thornborough (Bucks). (Source: J. A. Mills).

Their perception of the nearest available service was obviously different from that of the main settlement in the same parish (Fig 7.2).

However, given provisos such as these, the directories can indicate broadly the kind of interdependence which existed between villages. In order to remove the complications of immediate competition from a market town, two examples have been chosen where the village under study is completely surrounded by rural parishes. Hence, a fifth proviso is that we should always remember the strong attraction which any nearby market town could exert on the purses of country folk.

A Buckinghamshire example

Table 7.1 is based on an arbitrary list of 12 services which it is assumed the inhabitants of Nash required from time to time, only four of which were available in that village in 1891. The small village of Thornton was able to offer nothing, whilst Beachampton only had a pub, and Nash was already provided for in that respect. Therefore, short of going to Stony Stratford or Buckingham, the people of Nash had to turn to one of its other four neighbours for the eight 'missing' services. Great Horwood was the only one

67

Table 7.1 Village interdependence: Nash (Bucks) and neighbours, 1891

Village & Population	Nash 306	Beachampton 181	Whaddon 398	Lt. Horwood 304	Gt. Horwood 639	Thornbro 564
Service						
Baker	X				X	X
Blacksmith	X				X	X
Bootmaker					X	
Builder			X		X	X
Butcher					X	X
Carpenter			X		X	X
Grocer			X	X	X	
Public House	X	X	X	X	X	X
Saddler					X	
Shopkeeper	X			X	X	X
Tailor					X	
Wheelwright			X		X	X

Note: Thornton, with a population of 80, had no services and has therefore been left out of the table.

Source: Kelly's *Directory of Buckinghamshire*, 1891.

which offered all of them, but there was a choice of three villages with builders, and two villages each in the case of bakers, butchers, carpenters and grocers. This left Great Horwood with no competition in bootmaking, saddlery and tailoring.

It is important to recognise that the traffic was potentially a two-way flow between villages of similar size. Thus, for example, Nash people may have gone to Whaddon, the nearest other village, for a builder, carpenter, grocer or wheelwright, but they could offer in return the services of a baker and a blacksmith, which Whaddon lacked. Hence, it is appropriate to use the term interdependence, rather than dependence, although it is also clear from the table that some villages were more dependent than others.

A Leicestershire example

The second example is also taken, for the sake of simplicity, from an area of lowland England with closely spaced villages, and away from the direct influence of a market town. (Readers may wish to compare these two examples with villages situated next to market towns, and perhaps more interestingly with areas in the country in which true villages were widely spaced, such as the Fens, the Welsh uplands, and parts of the Pennines.) In the Leicestershire example, the range of services examined has been widened to include schools and nonconformist churches.

Table 7.2   Village interdependence: Ashby Folville (Leics) and neighbours, 1863

Village & Population	Ashby 160	Gaddesby 341	Thorpe Satchville 171	Twyford 372	Barsby 290
Service					
Baker		X		X	X
Beerhouse			X	X	
Blacksmith			X	X	X
Bootmaker		X		X	X
Bricklayer		X		X	
Butcher		X	X	X	X
Carpenter/Joiner	X	X	X		X
C of E church	X	X	X	X	
Cooper		X			
Grocer		X			
Miller	X			X	
Nonconformist Chapel (Wesleyan)		X		X	X
Plumber					X
Public House	X	X		X	X
Saddler				X	
School		X	X	X	X
School (Wesleyan)				X	
Shopkeeper	X		X	X	X
Tailor		X	X	X	X
Wheelwright		X		X	

Source: White's *Directory of Leicestershire and Rutland*, 1863.

The first comment to make is that there was a broad correspondence between population and service levels, as common sense would suggest (Table 7.2). Nevertheless, the biggest village did not have a complete set of the services represented in the table. Twyford was short of a plumber, grocer, cooper and carpenter/joiner, the most surprising being the latter, unless the wheelwright undertook joinery work as well. And at the other extreme, lowly Ashby, with its miller, could offer to three villages in the group something they lacked. Widening out the table to include non-commercial services brings into discussion other ways in which one can trace interdependence between neighbouring villages. For instance Barsby, which lay in the parish of Ashby Folville, had no church or Anglican chapel-of-ease, so we should imagine the lane between Barsby and Ashby busy with the passage of churchgoers on Sundays. Nonconformists might expect to travel further, there being only three Wesleyan chapels in the five villages, and none for other denominations. This theme can be followed up in nonconformist records, where, for example, lists of trustees and baptismal and burial registers sometimes give places of residence; and the Methodist circuit plans indicate how preachers moved around within a district. Parish registers are likewise sometimes useful in showing intermarriage between villages, and that burials and baptisms frequently involved non-residents too.

Indeed, the directories themselves can sometimes yield evidence of other links between villages which concerned the established church. Even where each village had its own place of Anglican worship, the congregrations might share a priest, especially where population levels were low. A case in point are five Lincolnshire villages a few miles west and north-west of the small market town of Horncastle, which were served by the Rev. John Fawssett. The 1892 edition of Crockford's Clerical Directory indicates that Fawssett was rector of Waddingworth 1843–91, vicar of Great Sturton with Baumber (two churches) 1849–91 and rector of Gautby, 1887–91. For the situation on the ground in any particular year, however, the county directories are rather more reliable. White's 1842, Hagar's 1849 and White's 1856 between them indicate that Fawssett was living in Horncastle in the early 1840s, like many contemporary rural clergy, who preferred the comforts and society of town to the wilds of rural Lincolnshire. In addition to the livings mentioned above, Fawssett was also curate of Minting for many years, going to live in the vicarage house there newly built in the 1840s, in a relatively large village in the centre of the area he served.

Schools were sometimes another kind of meeting point for villages. In Nottinghamshire, two pairs of villages, Sutton and Lound, and North and South Clifton, shared schools built about halfway between the villages. At Winthorpe in the same county the school was built at the very northern end of the village street for the convenience of children coming the opposite way from the smaller village of Langford (see Fig. 3.1 for a further example).

Going back to the Leicestershire example, Ashby and Barsby shared the school in Barsby, where the greater population lay. Children from South Croxton, one mile on the opposite side of Barsby, also went to school there according to the 1863 directory. Parents requiring more specialised education for their children clearly had to send them further afield, perhaps to board, but a sufficient example exists in Table 7.2, where Twyford is seen as the only village in the group with a school which specifically followed the doctrines of the Wesleyan denomination.

Charities were a further area in which there might be inter-village connections. Again our study area of Leicestershire provides an appropriate illustration. Under Twyford, White noted in 1863 that the income from Woollaston's Charity was divided among the poor of six parishes: two-tenths each to Twyford, South Croxton, Billesdon and Barsby, and one-tenth each to Lowesby and Cold Overton. The acting trustee, Sir Frederick Fowke, Bart, of Lowesby must have had a tricky time overseeing fairplay. Churches, chapels, charities and schools do not exhaust the activities in which there was interdependence between villages, but they are probably the most obvious topics on which to seek information in directories, other than commercial activities.

CHAPTER EIGHT

TOWN AND COUNTRY

My father was the village carrier and he took his cart to Buckingham four days a week to bring back the needs of the village. The fare for passengers was 2d single, 3d return. He would bring 12 to 14 dozen *Buckingham Advertisers* to sell for 1d each, of which he received a farthing commission.
— Tommy Whitehall, in *Thornborough parish magazine*, 1984.

Village dependence on towns

From village interdependence the scene moves on to the dependence of country on town. This can be explained in terms of the advantage which market towns possessed over even the most self-sufficient villages. There were more outlets and practitioners in the towns, with the result that competition kept prices down and standards up. On market days, the presence of stalls selling produce, crockery, clothing, footwear and many household requisites intensified the competition. Farmers were attracted by cattle markets (Fig. 8.1). Commercial fairs were still being held in towns at dates when they had only an entertainment value in villages. These were important additional outlets for farm produce from the surrounding countryside, and sometimes for buying in stock from distant areas, for example, young cattle or sheep for winter fattening. Some fairs were associated with the hiring of labour (statute fairs), attracting large numbers of prospective employees and farmers, all bent on striking a good bargain and having a drink on it.

The inns were hard pressed on such days to keep up with the extra trade, since they already had trade of a kind that was absent or much less prevalent in village hostelries. This included meeting the needs of vehicles and riders who wanted changes of horses and refreshment for themselves. Many inn-yards were the places where country carriers put up their covered carts for the day, while they were running errands in the town for their country clientele. Although through road traffic declined with the coming of the railways, the activities of the carriers increased, partly because the towns were often railheads for neighbouring villages. Towards the end of the century cyclists would 'put up' their cycles in pub-yards, and the *Queen Commercial Hotel* in Lincoln High Street was still providing this facility in the late 1940s. Similarly, the *Lion Hotel*, in the same street, had moved with the times by renting its yard to the Lincolnshire Road Car Company as a bus station, a trend emulated elsewhere.

Fig. 8.1. The *Imperial Gazetteer* said of St. Ives (Hunts) that 'A weekly market is held on Monday; and well-frequented fairs are held on Whit-Monday and 11 Oct'. This photograph shows the reality of Mondays around 1890. Shopkeepers would be in two minds about the benefits of the cattle market — more trade, but more 'nuisances'. The mess and congestion had already persuaded most larger towns to remove cattle markets from their streets by this date, using a yard by the station or a field on the outskirts of the town instead. However, it was not until the middle of the twentieth century that the practice of driving animals to market through the streets finally ceased. (Source: Cambridgeshire County Record Office, Huntingdon).

Perhaps most importantly, towns could offer goods and services of a specialist kind which one only met with very occasionally in villages. Many of these services were associated with professions, such as architects, attorneys and the courts, auction yards and salerooms, banking, doctors (and dentists at later dates), grammar schools, and insurance agencies. More sophisticated leisure facilities were also to be found in the towns, including theatres, concert halls, libraries, and in later years professional football and cinematograph halls. Also towards 1900 commercial and public business became more complex, requiring office blocks for the headquarters of companies (for example, Co-operative Societies, which often had rural branches), for the Head Post Offices (including early telephone exchanges) and for the central administrations of the new rural district councils and county councils.

Such facilities and services were clearly an attraction for country people, especially those in the higher social groups, whose income and way of life both demanded and made possible regular visits to towns. Property-owners went to lawyers, grocers to wholesale houses, wives and husbands to the furniture emporiums providing a delivery service. The directories would have facilitated such activities, as the *Yellow Pages* do today.

The lower income groups depended much more on the carriers' carts, the carriers taking passengers as well as collecting goods for villagers. Townsfolk would ride out to see country relatives: the author's father recalled travelling in the carrier's cart from Lincoln to Willoughton, a distance of about 14 miles, in order to stay with his grandmother during the school holidays just before the First World War. Some carriers, as well as waggons in pre-railway days, ran between towns of different sizes, since all but the largest town, London, had some dependence on others higher up the urban hierarchy. Thus, Berridge Cragg, of West Street, Sleaford, Lincolnshire, ran every Tuesday, Thursday and Saturday morning to the *Blue Ram* in Grantham, returning at 3 pm. His advertisement in the *Sleaford Gazette Almanack* for 1874 says 'Passengers receive every attention. Parcels and Commissions faithfully attended to'.

The *Sleaford Gazette Almanack*: a market town and its villages

Annual almanacs published locally generally contained some directory-type information, but the *Sleaford Gazette* was possibly unusual in setting out to provide a 'Directory of the Neighbourhood' with its almanac. Perhaps the large size of Lincolnshire meant that local publishers could produce what many people needed at a fraction of the cost of a whole-county directory. It is also worth noting that in publishing a directory the newspaper office was making a second use of much information it had collected for journalistic and advertising purposes, whilst the almanac helped to advertise the newspaper.

The *Sleaford Gazette Almanack* records the kinds of attractions that Sleaford, with a population of only 3,600, afforded the villages in its vicinity. They included six solicitors, four medical men, a grammar school, three banks, four auctioneers, six chemists and druggists, four cabinet makers and upholsterers, three curriers (curers of leather), two coach builders, three ironmongers, four printers, three photographers, three servants' register offices, two taxidermists, and three inland revenue officers! There were also one each of the following: pianoforte tuner (also the church organist), architect, basket maker, corset maker, dyer, game dealer, gunsmith, millwright and engineer, nail maker, and surveyor.

The village entries printed in this almanac cannot compare with those in the regular directories, there being no parish descriptions save the latest population figure, and the lists of inhabitants look somewhat perfunctory. However, the contrasts between villages come out clearly enough (Fig. 8.2), as also between all of them and Sleaford.

The *Almanack* can also lead us into a study of the hinterland or market area of the town. Carrier services are one relevant criterion and these appear in most, but not all, directories, often in two places — once under villages, once under a town. In the case of this almanac, the carriers' list under Sleaford includes 40

KELBY.

Population : 87.

Barrand, Mrs., farmer
Bailey, Robert, joiner
Briggs, H., cottager
Duffin, John cottager
Everitt, William, farmer
Matkin, John, farmer

Nixon, Henry, farmer
Pinder, Joseph, farmer
Pinder, — farmer
Sandy, George, farmer
Skerritt, Job, cottager
Wetherell, David, cottager

SPANBY.

Population : 115

Ato, Thomas, farmer
Bellamy, Dawson, farmer
Cropley, Crosby, farmer

Dodsworth, John, farmer
Horseman, Thomas, farmer
Hardstaff, Joseph, farmer

Lunn, Speed, parish clerk

WILSFORD.

Population : 647.

Younge, Rev. J. P. B , rector
Allen, John, grocer and draper
Allen, John, carpenter
Ash, Samuel, Plough Inn
Bell, Joseph, tailor
Bemrose, J. H., farmer
Blankney, Thos., farmer, Hanbeck
Clarkson, James, greengrocer
Dennis, Matthew, parish clerk
Grey, Brothers, Wilsford Warren
Gostick, Joseph, cordwainer
Hutchinson, Thos., miller and baker
Martin, John, Marquis of Granby

Mason, John, cordwainer & grocer
Parkinson, Thomas, farmer
Parkinson, J. H., the Hall
Palmer, Miss independent
Patchett, Joseph, butcher
Peach, John, farmer
Rimmington, James, Rutland Arms
Rowlett, Mrs., dressmaker
Slight, George, farmer
Smith, Matthew, cattle dealer
Theaker, C , farmer, the Valley
Thornby, Dean, wheelwright
Unwin, Edwin, schoolmaster

HOWELL.

Population : 86.

Dolby, Rev. John S., rector
Dudding, J. W., esq.
Parr, — farmer

Sardeson, Henry, farmer
Foster, — parish clerk

QUARRINGTON.

Population : 340.

Shannon, Rev. F, T , rector
Bacon, Mrs. G.
Cubley, Mrs., farmer
Clements, Miss
Clark, John, cottager
Edwards, Wm,, refreshment rooms
Fisher, John, cottager
Fox, John, beerhouse
Heald, Mrs.
Jefferies, Hezekiah, grocer
Jackson, Mrs , cottager
Jackson, Robert, cottager

Key, William, cottager
Key, Richard, cottager
Mowbray, Wm.
Noble, James, cottager
Oliver, Rev. J. H., Wesleyan Reform Minister
Pullen, W., parish clerk and sexton
Taylor, William, cottager
Todkill, Robert, cottager
Struggles, W., shoemaker
Ward, F., farmer

Fig. 8.2. Page 27 of the *Sleaford Gazette Almanack* for 1874 demonstrates how the publisher packed in small villages to gain maximum attention for a minimum outlay. The three smallest were too small to sustain any tradesman or craftsman. The term 'cottager', very prevalent on this page, was used in Lincolnshire and Nottinghamshire, not of labourers but of men with cottage farms. Cross reference to census enumerators' books shows that they generally had between about 5 and 20 acres. Their houses and outbuildings were in scale. Elsewhere the term 'smallholder' was often used.

Fig. 8.3. G.A. Simpson was the carrier at Folkingham (Lincs) c. 1910s and plied to three different market towns: Grantham, Sleaford and Bourne. The windows and the cases on the roof indicate that he was in the habit of carrying passengers. (Source: Local Studies Collection, Lincoln Central Library, by courtesy of Lincolnshire County Council, Education and Cultural Services Directorate). On occasion, carriers' journeys could be hazardous. For example, Simpson probably approached Grantham down Somerby Hill, now the A52, which is very steep. On 25 May 1907 a van similar to his overturned after the horse bolted, killing three people and seriously injuring others. The excitement attracted a photographer who published post-cards of the accident scene, now in the Eric Croft Collection.

destinations served by carriers and mail carts. When a town had the status of post town the area for which it acted in that capacity can also be used as a means of defining its hinterland. As today, this involved the delivery of mails to country areas and their collection for outward dispatch. The routing of mails usually appears in the parish entries of county directories, in some such phrase as 'Letters via Colsterworth' or 'Post from Truro'. Corresponding information usually appears in town entries for the whole of the town's postal district. The *Sleaford Gazette Almanack* printed the daily journeys undertaken by Post Office Messengers, and the times of receipt and dispatch of letters are also given.

Similar lists of villages can be found under other administrative heads, such as Poor Law Unions, which ran the workhouses and dispensed relief in various forms. The Sleaford Poor Law Union contained no less than 58 rural parishes. So much can be found in most county directories, but the *Sleaford Gazette Almanack* is unusual in that it implicitly reveals the area in which the *Gazette* itself regularly circulated, since it included information on 74 villages, an area much bigger than the Poor Law Union. Coincidentally, 1874 was the year in which the Venerable Archdeacon Trollope published his book on the history of Sleaford and the surrounding parishes, and the advertisement for it shows that the indefatigable parson had drawn a line at 44 parishes. Clearly, it is impossible to draw a single line to demarcate the edge of a town's hinterland.

Carriers

Carriers like Mr Whitehall of Thornborough (see head of chapter) were an absolutely vital link between village and town, especially for ordinary folk without their own horse-drawn transport. Another recollection of an individual carrier is that of Mr Cooper Allwood of Wellingore near Lincoln, who used to leave the village at 7.45 am on a Friday morning, using a small silver-coloured horn to let villagers know of his approach. By about midday he had covered the 10 miles to Lincoln, having stopped in intermediate villages. The *Horse and Jockey* was the main collection point in Waddington, and here Mr Allwood would take hot soup on a winter's day. His horse-drawn cart was withdrawn from service in 1928, when Mr Buckberry started a lorry service for goods, passengers having transferred to the Silver Queen bus service (see also Fig 8.4).[1]

Although long-distance waggons were put out of business by the railways, carriers' carts multiplied in the Victorian period on most short-distance routes connecting the countryside with the nearest towns and some of the railway stations. Those employed in the carrying trade in England and Wales rose from about 82,000 in 1851 to 273,000 in 1901.[2] It should be added that deliveries were sometimes carried out by town shops and suppliers sending out horse-drawn vans into the countryside, but this appears to have been mainly a development of the motor era, after the First World War. Among the operators the Co-operative Societies were prominent, and so accepted a part of rural life it had become that a restricted service was continued during the Second World War, when petrol supplies were scarce and ageing vehicles difficult to maintain.

Among the substantial studies of carriers is that of the Bristol region, based mainly on Kelly's 1897 *Directory of the Counties of Somerset and Gloucester, with the City of Bristol*. With a population of about 340,000, Bristol was a magnet for carriers from a ring of villages extending about 20 miles out from the city and containing a population of about 160,000. Morgan describes their usual functions of taking agricultural produce to market, carrying passengers, and acting as shopping agents for village people. Among the consignments going out from Bristol were supplies of cloth destined for seamstresses and tailoresses in Winterbourne and Watley's End, who made waistcoats and jackets and sent them back to Bristol by the same carriers.

Conditions of travel are also described by Morgan, including early starts and late returns, unpleasant on dark winter roads. The surfaces had no waterproof metalling, at the best comprising 'stone bound with dust and water sprayed with a film of tar'. Progress was slow, the six miles from Winterbourne to Bristol taking about three hours. It is remarkable that of the 498 hotels, inns and taverns in the city in 1897, the carriers concentrated at only 13 hostelries.

Fig. 8.4. This carefully stage-managed picture shows four forms of transport in the early 1920s, of which the bus is the centrepiece and probably the latest innovation. The others include a 28-inch wheel bicycle; a motor-cycle, probably belt-driven and pre-1914; and a Model T Ford in the distance. Kelly's *Directory of Lincolnshire*, 1922 recorded William Edward Balderson as carrier, cycle agent and motor engineer, which seems to match the location; BP petrol is advertised for sale as well as the ubiquitous Colman's Starch. Brigg, Market Rasen, Lincoln and Grimsby were reached by carriers' carts before the bus intervened. (Source: Maurice Hodson Post-card Collection).

These were located in central shopping streets, specialised in providing stabling, oats and water for the horses, and had parking space between them for the 344 services operating over the course of a week. Most of the 93 carriers operated services several times weekly, so that carrying was usually a full-time occupation, but 18 dual-occupationists were traced. Their secondary occupations were mostly 'connected with the licensing trade, with agricultural tasks, or with the ownership of vehicles providing related services; but this is not surprising since carriers' work impinged on all three areas'.[3]

It is necessary to be very careful in the identification of carrier services, and Morgan states that although using the Bristol section of the 1897 directory for most of his information, he also checked the village entries, and added carriers to Kelly's list by cross-checking with Wright's directory of the same year. Accordingly, the remainder of this chapter comprises a similar exercise for a small group of Lincolnshire villages.

Carriers: a Lincolnshire example

These villages are situated in an area in which the hinterlands of three market towns overlapped (Fig 8.6). The exercise is based on one of the best Lincolnshire directories, that published in 1892 by William White. Despite this, a significant

Fig. 8.5. J. E. White, the carrier between Yatton and Bristol, one of those studied by Kenneth Morgan in *Country carriers*. (Source: Bristol Branch, Historical Association).

number of discrepancies are revealed between village entries and those for the towns of Boston, Spilsby and Horncastle.[4] Carriers appeared twice over in most village entries, both in the alphabetical listings and in a separate statement, such as that under New Bolingbroke: 'Carriers - Charles Stennett and William Baker to Boston, Wed. and Sat'., but for Hameringham 'Carrier passes through to Horncastle on Saturdays' (see also Fig. 5.1 for an unusually detailed route).

Table 8.1 lists all entries for the nine villages in the study area. Some of the discrepancies are easily detected by comparing columns making up the pairs. For instance, running the eye down the Horncastle pair soon reveals that under Hameringham the town entry gives Greenfield's name, but the village entry is only the vague 'Carrier passes through to Horncastle on Saturdays'. Some such discrepancies may not be due to carelessness, but to changes in circumstances between two different dates of collecting information. For example, had Roberts of Mareham-le-Fen given up his cart after the Horncastle entry was made up and before the agent reported on the village? The most serious discrepancy concerns Stennett and Baker of New Bolingbroke: the village entry suggests they went to Boston on Saturdays as well as on Wednesdays, but the Horncastle town entry sensibly contradicts this by suggesting that it was Horncastle on Saturdays (its market days) rather than Boston. However, the Boston town entry gives out another discordant note to the effect that Baker went there on Wednesdays, Thursdays and Saturdays. The Boston entry also seemingly misplaces Evison of Mareham-le-Fen under New Bolingbroke, whilst the entry under Scrivelsby appears to be completely anomalous.

Table 8.1 Carriers from villages lying to south-east of Horncastle, Lincs, 1892

Village and 1891 population	To Horncastle Saturday	From Horncastle Saturday	To Boston Wednesday	From Boston Wednesday	To Spilsby Monday	From Spilsby Monday
East Kirkby 319	Thompson	Thompson	CPT Packet boat also Sats	Packet boat also Sats	CPT	
Hameringham 144	CPT	Greenfield				
Mareham-le-Fen 803	Coupland Evison Major	Coupland Evison Major Roberts	Evison Major	Abbot Major	Coupland	Coupland
Mareham-on-the-Hill 126	CPT					
Miningsby 101	CPT					
Moorby 75						
New Bolingbroke 401		Baker Stennett	Baker Stennett both also Sats	Baker, also Thu & Sats Stennett Evison		Baker
Revesby 516	CPT	Burn	CPT	(Lanley to H'castle)	CPT	
Scrivelsby 127	CPT					
Wood Enderby 147						

Note: Carrier services *to* each town are taken from the village entries, whilst those *from* each town are taken from the appropriate town entries. The packet boat connecting East Kirkby and Boston started and finished its journey at Hagnaby Lock, one-and-a-half miles from the village and sailed via the West Fen Catchwater Drain and the Stone Bridge Drain. CPT = carriers pass through (a standard entry followed by the name of a town and the day(s) of the week).

Source: White's *Directory of Lincolnshire*, 1892.

This exercise makes plain that the exact routes and a complete set of stopping places of individual carriers are not recorded. For example, Burn of Revesby may have travelled to Horncastle via Moorby or Mareham-le-Fen, but at least the directory does fill in some of the blank spaces by recording that unnamed carriers passed through the smaller villages, except for Wood Enderby and Moorby. The broad picture of better services for the bigger villages confirms what common sense would suggest. The fact that villages often had a choice of market town is also well illustrated here, as it applied to four of the ten villages. A particular feature of interest in this area is that carrier services by road were supplemented by a packet boat on the fen drains connecting East Kirkby with Boston. Even at this late date, fifty years after the railways were first being built, some packet boat services were surviving out of the much larger numbers available in mid-century in many parts of the country, including coastwise services.

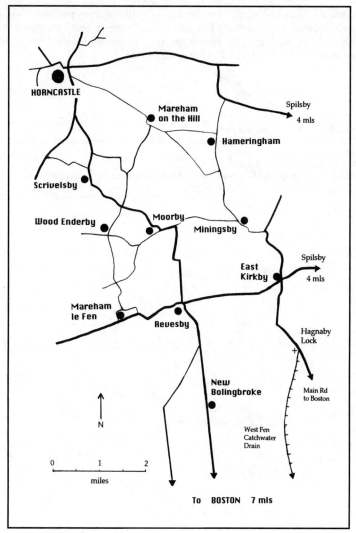

Fig. 8.6. Map to illustrate carrier routes in the area south-east of Horncastle (Lincs), 1892. (Source: J. A. Mills).

In addition to discrepancies within what appear to be reliable directories, the historian is also in danger from a few directories that give so little information on carriers as to be useless. Kelly's directories for Hertfordshire published in 1850 and 1890 are a particular case in point. So anyone bent on a special study of carriers needs to forage around at some length before settling on a choice of directories.

This chapter concludes the discussion of village communities and the economic relationships both within and between them, and between villages and towns. The next chapter moves on to a countywide scenario, a wider context in which to evaluate what has gone before.

NOTES

1. *Lincolnshire Chronicle*, 5 February 1971.
2. Chartres, 'Country tradesmen', 301. Only about half that number were country carriers, compare with Chapter 6, page 57.
3. Morgan, *Country carriers*, especially 10–12.
4. Moreau, *Departed village*, 136, reports similar discrepancies for his Oxfordshire village.

CHAPTER 9

USING COUNTY LISTS

Yellow Pages brings in business: when people are ready to buy they turn to *Yellow Pages*. – part of an advertisement in *Yellow Pages*.

The lists described, using a Dorset example

County lists are available in the later directories of the nineteenth century and those of the early twentieth. To illustrate their potential, Kelly's *Directory of Dorsetshire* for 1920 is used as the main example in the first part of this chapter. Pages 1–20 of this directory comprise general information about the county, including, among other topics, details of the registration districts, poor law unions, hundreds and liberties, MPs and military information; fairs, markets and crops; Dorset County Council; JPs for the county (earlier editions would have listed gentlemen's seats); County Police; and the geology of Dorset. Whilst these introductory pages contain lists of names for the county, these are not the 'county lists' with which this chapter is concerned. Pages 21–258 contain the A–Z gazetteer of town and village entries, and then on page 259 the county lists begin and continue up to the end of the main text 110 pages later.

There are two of these lists, one an A–Z list of private residents (see Appendix 9.1), the other a series of A–Z lists for each of the trades and professions identified in the gazetteer section. This is headed 'Dorsetshire Trades and Professional Directory' and this kind of list is of much greater use to rural community historians. There are, of course, the usual problems of classification, which anyone familiar with the *Yellow Pages* is unlikely to overlook. For instance, smiths, blacksmiths and farriers are listed together, but jobbing gardeners, private gardeners, landscape gardeners, market gardeners, and nurserymen and seedsmen all occur separately (see Fig. 9.1). However, there is no reason to suppose that the lists contain any marked bias in terms of comprehensiveness and accuracy as between one part of the county and another.

One advantage of the county trades lists arises in studies requiring total numbers in each trade or the distribution over a county of particular trades and services. Thus in principle the decline of a trade can be traced through successive editions of Kelly's directories, provided there is evidence of reasonable consistency of definitions over the period studied. This cannot be guaranteed, however, as the later example of ploughmaking indicates.

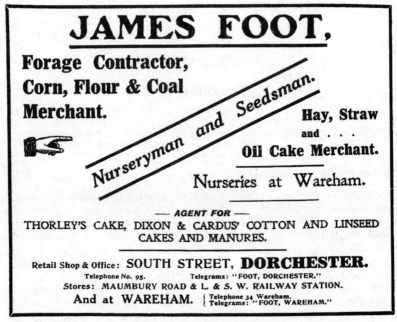

Fig. 9.1. An example of an advertisement found in Kelly's *Directory of Dorsetshire*, 1920. James Foot shows yet again how varied enterprises often were in this period. Many directories carried advertisements from outside the areas to which they related, just as in our *Yellow Pages*.

As in the case of family history, the directories can be used as convenient starting points for local investigations relative to a trade. A good example might be milling, since mills, more than most rural enterprises, tend to leave traces on the ground long after they have been closed down. In 1920 there were 70 milling enterprises in Dorset, mostly watermills, but one used steam only, and six used steam as a supplement to waterpower. A Lincolnshire man finds it hard to believe that not a single windmill was working in Dorset at that date. Armed with a list of approximate locations, the industrial archaeologist could then turn to Ordnance Survey maps and go in search of the remains of the watermills of Dorset. Earlier lists would be more complete, but would contain a larger proportion of mills that have been demolished.

The range of goods and services available to a county in a particular period can be of considerable help to the historian in building up a period-picture, or in providing an appropriate context for various studies. Advertisements from outside the county can also be expected for some of the more specialised services, or those able to compete by mail order. Among the unusual and/or newer products and services available in Dorset in 1920 were the following, with numbers of entries in brackets:

Aerodrome (1)	Hurdle makers (12)
Agricultural tractors (1)	Jam manufacturer (1)
Bacon and ham curers (2)	Millwrights (2)
Caseine & dried milk manufacturer (1)	Motor car proprietors (18)
Cinematograph halls (16)	Poultry appliance manufacturer (1)
Damp-proof course manufacturer (1)	Rabbit skin merchant (1)
Egg merchants (7)	Reading and newsrooms (32)
Electric light companies (5)	Servants' registry offices (4)
Flax growers (5)	Tractor and plough contractor (1)
Fruit preserver (1)	Watercress growers (2)
Horticultural builder (1)	Well borer and sinker (1)

Ploughmakers in the East Midlands

A preliminary point to note in this case study is that most large agricultural engineers were located in towns, one advantage being proximity to the cattle markets that brought farmers into towns. Some factories were even large by modern standards, Ransomes of Ipswich, for example, having an international market. Nevertheless some village manufacturers (as opposed to agents and repairers) kept going into the twentieth century, the firm of R. T. Reeves and Son Ltd of Bratton, near Trowbridge, Wilts, being a well documented example.[1] Bealbys of Collingham near Newark were basically wheelwrights, craftsmen in wood, who bought in most of the metal parts for the wooden ploughs they built themselves. Collingham was, and is, a big village, with a station on the Midland line from Lincoln to Derby and an agricultural show and ploughing match of its own. Otherwise it was less well placed for plough manufacture than the average market town (Figs. 9.2 and 9.3).

Work on the Bealby account books for the 1870s revealed that more plough customers farmed in the mixed or basically grassland areas of central and western Nottinghamshire, of Derbyshire and south Yorkshire, than in the arable farming districts of Lincolnshire which are situated close to Collingham in the opposite direction (eastwards). Whilst the railway pattern may have had some bearing on this lopsided distribution of customers, it is probably more to do with the location of other plough manufacturers. At this point in the work, recourse was made to directories.

The directories for the West Riding and the East Midland counties begin to contain county lists of plough makers and agricultural implement manufacturers during the 1850s. A search of the relevant Kelly's and White's directories produced an indication that Bealbys were selling 'away' from their main rivals located in the arable areas of Lincolnshire,

Fig. 9.2. Frank Bealby of Collingham (Notts) in the early 1980s, showing his grandfather's last plough, made in the 1920s just before the firm closed. Frank spent most of his working life at Ransome and Marles, the ball-bearing manufacturers in nearby Newark, the kind of firm to which many village craftsmen gravitated at this time. In the background is one of the workshops. (Source: Peter Morrell).

where there must have been a heavier demand for the product, but equally more competition.

Between 1860 and 1881 few ploughmakers were found west of Collingham, despite the availability of various types of iron and steel in Derbyshire and the Don Valley. Presumably areas such as Lincolnshire, stimulated by the local market, developed the appropriate technologies. Among other developments, this involved the replacement of wood by iron and steel, a process which appears to have been gradual, and which led to Bealbys' predominantly wooden ploughs competing with all-metal ploughs at the opposite end of the range. The larger works were Richard Hornsby and Sons Ltd of Grantham and John Cooke in Lincoln, who could afford advertisements in directories, both those for Lincolnshire and those for counties further afield. Also in Lincoln was Charles Duckering who manufactured plough shares.

The nature of the directory entries themselves is problematical because of a change in classification, but they suggest that the industry was undergoing restructuring. The directories of the 1850s and 1860s used the separate title 'ploughmakers', but later directories included them in the list of agricultural implement makers, indicating an interest in plough manufacture only by

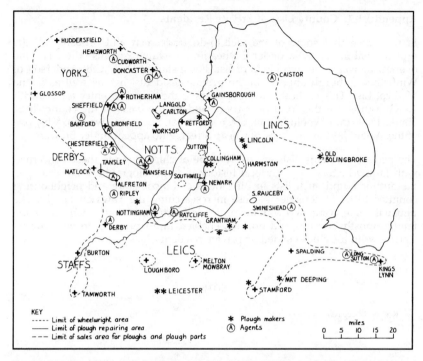

Fig. 9.3. Location map of specialist plough-makers in the West Riding and the East Midlands, based on an accumulated list compiled from White's and Kelly's directories for the period 1860–81 by Miss M. Andrews. The three areas delimited by lines indicate the three kinds of work carried out by Bealbys. The agents shown were those selling for Bealbys. (Source: D. R. Mills)

means of an asterisk against each appropriate name. Eventually the asterisks disappear and plough-making can only be tracked down through advertisements. How much this disappearance is due to re-classification, and how much to restructuring of the industry is difficult to tell. However, it is clear that the independent, specialist ploughmakers did eventually disappear in the face of competition from the big agricultural engineering companies with diversified interests. One factor in this process, at least as far as the Bealbys were concerned, was the gradual evolution of an all-metal plough, Ransomes being literally one of the first in the field with this development. As workers in wood, the Bealbys found themselves buying in more and more metal parts, usually from the Sheffield area, until the balance was so unfavourable to wood that the basis of their operation completely disappeared in the 1920s.

This brief account of plough-making indicates the potential uses to which county lists can be put, helping the historian to place his individual community and its trades in a much wider and more secure context.

Appendix 9.1: County Lists of Private Residents

In the sense that some of the well-to-do tradesmen and probably all the professional men appear under the heading 'private residents', there is some overlap between the two kinds of list. For instance, Dr M.C.B. Anderson of Winfrith Newburgh appears in the private residents' list, as well as in the Medical List. This replicates what appears in the gazetteer entry for Winfrith Newburgh, since this kind of entry would be the basis of the county lists. Similarly, Arthur Woolmington, of Cheap Street, Sherborne was probably one of the Woolmington Brothers, of Cheap Street, who appear under Brewers.

The private residents' lists are likely to be of chief value to those concerned with family history, or with local history through biographies. For example, the author found such lists in directories of Lincolnshire and neighbouring counties to be of considerable use in researching the Fawssett family. The unusual name, combined with the professional status of many members of the family, mostly parsons and doctors, enabled rapid progress to be made by starting with the clues yielded by private residents' lists.

NOTE

1. Reeves, Sheep *bell and ploughshare*.

CHAPTER TEN

PARISH DESCRIPTIONS, GLOSSARY and EPILOGUE

Compton Gifford, a tything in Charles-the-Martyr parish, Devon; one-and-a-half miles NNE of Plymouth. It includes the small villages of Compton, Mannamead, Mutley and Hyde Park terrace, comprising a number of fine residences; and has a post office, of the name of Compton, under Plymouth. Acres, 641...Pop. 880, Houses, 140...   – Wilson, *The Imperial Gazetteer*, 1870 edn, 480.

The Imperial Gazetteers

That directories have to be used with some care must now be well appreciated. Parish descriptions have to be treated with the usual caution, and they are much less standardised than the parish lists of residents. However, they are more easily cross-checked against other sources than are residents' lists, with the consequence that suspicion as to their accuracy is more easily aroused. This chapter aims to help readers to get the most out of parish descriptions without taking too many risks, and to further this objective by explaining some of the technical terms which were used, and the contexts in which the descriptions were written.

As they cover the whole of England and Wales, and are confined to descriptive material, it is convenient to begin with the *Imperial Gazetteers*, an extract from one of which can be seen at the chapter head. Although not widely available, the *Gazetteers* can be found in some reference libraries and record offices. In addition to parish descriptions, they conveniently contain entries on landscape features, such as Easdale, a mountain vale in Westmorland; Compton Bay in the Isle of Wight; Coney Beds, a Roman 'camp' near Kendal; the River Conder, a tributary of the River Lune; and Eldon Hole, a cavern near Castleton. Also appearing as separate entries are some country seats, like Compton Place, the seat of the Duke of Devonshire in Sussex; railway lines such as the Cheshire Midland Railway and the East Anglian Railway; and some hundreds, such as the East and West Easwrith Hundreds in Sussex. Each county is also the subject of several pages of description. The last volume in the alphabetically arranged series concludes with a summary of national information of a statistical kind taken from government papers, including the latest census.

The parish or township descriptions are similar to those found in directories, of varying length and types of information. Some of the topics that may be mentioned include: location, geographical and administrative information, acreage, annual value of real estate, population and number of houses at the last census, landownership and manorial rights, the living (its value, patron and church), charities, chapels, schools, post office, railway facilities in the area, outstanding historical events and remains, commercial activities, chief residences, and landscape features.

A Leicestershire example: open and closed villages

Despite the reservations, parish descriptions are very good for overall contrasts between different types of village, such as industrial or mining, compared with purely agricultural villages; or contrasts between the 'true' villages of the English Midlands and the scattered settlements of areas such as the Weald, the Chilterns or the Fens. The example chosen to illustrate contrasts comes from Leicestershire, a county in which the most important differences, especially within short distances, were those between 'open' and 'closed' villages. The extracts will almost define these terms for those to whom they are new, but broadly speaking 'closed' means a parish dominated by one owner and with restricted population growth, whilst 'open' is the reverse.[1] In this example Kirkby Mallory was a closed village, whilst its next door neighbour, Earl Shilton was open; up to 1854 they had constituted a single parish.

White's 1863 *Directory of Leicestershire* described Kirkby Mallory as a parish of 216 inhabitants and about 1,940 acres.

> The Earl Lovelace is lord of the manor, and owner of the soil, except one farm, belonging to Mr Thomas Jee; but his seat of Kirkby Mallory Hall is occupied by Baroness de Clifford... The Earl...is patron [of the living] and the Hon. and Rev. Augustus Byron, MA, son of the present Lord Byron, is the incumbent, and has a handsome residence...

In the list of residents for this village there are only 22 entries, including those of Lady Clifford's butler and gardener.

Contrast this description with that of Earl Shilton, which

> has many framework knitters' [stocking makers], and 'comprises about 1,980 acres, and 2,176 inhabitants [ten times as many as Kirkby Mallory on a similar acreage]. The Queen, as Duchess of Lancaster, is lady of the manor; but the rights thereof are reserved to the copyholders [customary tenants] themselves. The soil belongs to Thomas Wilkinson, George Allen, William Clark, and Thomas Atkins, Esqrs., several smaller proprietors and Alderman Newton's and other charities.

The residents' list has about 100 names, including four hosiery manufacturers (men who put out materials to the stockingers for making up), two framesmiths (who made and maintained the stocking frames or machines), nine innholders and tavern-keepers, and several less common trades, such as agricultural implement maker, watch and clock maker, harness maker and seed merchant, plumber, two druggists and two surgeons.

Perhaps the most important contrast between Earl Shilton and Kirkby Mallory lies in their population sizes, 2,176 and 216 respectively. Variations in community size have already been discussed in Chapters 3 and 4, and are exemplified in the directory entries reproduced in Figures 1.4, 4.2, 5.1 and 8.2, which may repay further study at this point. One is on safe ground with directories when sharp contrasts are apparent, since slight inaccuracies in detail are unlikely to distort the general view. However, where detail is significant, as in the study of a single village over time, the descriptions must be handled more cautiously. This point is now demonstrated by returning to Thornborough with the help of four directories, published by three different firms: Kelly's *Directories of Buckinghamshire*, 1848 and 1864, Craven and Musson's *Directory of Buckinghamshire*, 1853, and Cassey's *Directory of Buckinghamshire*, 1865.

The rest of this chapter is sub-divided by the various topics which appear in parish descriptions. Under each topic quotations are given from the Thornborough descriptions, not comprehensively from all four directories but selectively, in such a way as to highlight inconsistencies. Technical terms are discussed under the relevant topics, drawing in where necessary from other directories and other villages, in order to present most of the terms the reader is likely to encounter in most directories (see Figs. 6.1–6.2 for views of Thornborough; also Chapter 3 on large villages and small).

Geographical and administrative information

Craven and Musson 1853:

Thornborough is a village and parish, three miles east of Buckingham, and five miles west from Winslow, in the hundred and union of Buckingham, containing by the census of 1851, 754 inhabitants; and 2,500 acres of land...

Kelly 1864:

Thornborough is a large village and parish, three miles east of Buckingham, five north-north-west from Winslow, and 56 from London, in Buckingham hundred and archdeaconry, union, county court district, and rural deanery of Stony Stratford, and diocese of Oxford. The population in 1861 was 694; the area is 2,530 acres; the rateable value is £4,063.

General. Two general points to notice here are the inconsistency as to the direction of Thornborough from Winslow and the ambiguity in 1864 as to whether Thornborough was in the union and county court district of Buckingham or of Stony Stratford. Recourse to later directories suggests that either Thornborough was transferred backwards and forwards between the two towns, or had never left Buckingham, much the nearer town, for any purpose (see Fig. 7.2 for location map).

Village, hamlet. These terms are generally used to denote the chief centres of population in a parish. The distinction between them is partly one of size, but the term hamlet is sometimes used to indicate that a place was not an independent parish.

Parish. An area of land, and therefore a body of people, paying tithes and church rates for the upkeep of a parson and a church. In southern England, parish and township (for the latter, see below) usually coincided, but in the Midlands, and more particularly in northern England, where the medieval population was thinner on the ground, a parish might contain several townships and/or chapelries. For example, the *Imperial Gazetteer* of 1872 states that Bradford parish in the West Riding contained no less than 12 townships, in addition to Bradford itself, a total area of over 34,000 acres. The Leicestershire example of Earl Shilton, as a township in Kirkby Mallory parish until 1854, has already been mentioned. Appendix 4.1 discusses this topic in relation to the Billinghay group of townships (p. 41). (See also below, under **Religion**).

Extra-parochial places and liberties. These were areas exempt from parochial dues and often did not raise poor rates either, because of their status as former monastic properties, or portions of former royal or ducal forests.

Township. Not a town in our modern sense. A township was an area which had in former times possessed its own independent agricultural system, in many counties organised in open arable fields and areas of common pasture, meadow and 'waste'. The inhabited part of this communal entity was known as the 'town', typically a close grouping of farmsteads and cottages. The term 'market town' was used to distinguish towns that had acquired markets, and thereby urban status. During the late eighteenth and early nineteenth centuries the term 'town' came to be replaced in the rural context by the words 'village' and, occasionally, 'hamlet'.

Population. Usually taken from the previous census, but not always reliably so: for example, in 1848 Kelly gave Thornborough an 1841 population of 800, when the correct figure was 762. There is also scope for confusion between the figures for parish and township, in cases where the names, but not the areas, were coincident.

Area. The acreages were also taken from census reports, or from enclosure and tithe surveys, or from ratebooks. However, before the later decades of the nineteenth century, these sources were inclined to contradict each other, being based on different assumptions, such as the inclusion/exclusion of roads and water bodies. Also, surveying work could be of variable accuracy. Only towards the end of the century was the Ordnance Survey able to give the census authorities a complete set of accurate acreages for the whole country. For most counties they are easily accessible in *Victoria County History* population tables, and, of course, in later directories. Unless there is positive evidence of boundary changes, it is best to use the later figures for any date in the nineteenth century (see also Appendix 4.1).

Hundred, Wapentake, Soke, Tithing, Ward. These titles go back in various parts of the country to pre-Conquest times, but were still in use in the first half of the nineteenth century. Originally, they were groups of townships administered for purposes of defence, taxation, and law and order, each being under the supervision of a sheriff's officer, known variously as a high constable, tithingman and by other names, the townships having their own constables acting under him. From about the sixteenth century onwards the emphasis shifted towards the collection of taxes, such as Ship Money and land tax; and county rates, for example for bridges and prisons. Somewhat confusingly in some areas, the terms 'tithing' and 'ward' were used of portions of parishes, as in the modern use of ward for electoral purposes.

Poor Law Unions. The setting up of the Poor Law Unions, in most parts of the country in response to the Poor Law Amendment Act of 1834, was the first major breach in the traditional system of local government. The township, formerly solely responsible for the poor under the general jurisdiction of the JPs (magistrates), lost control to the Guardians of the Union and to the Union workhouse, often situated in a market town like Buckingham.

Petty Sessions, or divisional/district courts. It is from these courts that our present day magistrates' courts are directly descended. Minor cases, not warranting the attention of the Quarter Sessions, later the county courts, would come before the JPs, who dispensed justice without the aid of a jury, but with the assistance of their clerk, who was a local lawyer.

Rural deanery, archdeaconry. Rural Deans, as opposed to the deans of cathedrals, were (and are) senior parochial clergy who administered a group of their fellow clergymen working in an area somewhat similar in size to a hundred, sometimes with name and boundaries approximating to those of a hundred. Deaneries were grouped into archdeaconries, with an archdeacon in charge responsible to the diocesan bishop.

Summary. The directory publishers located a village within the various areas to which it belonged for administrative purposes, giving information useful to such as landowners, lawyers, clergy, and tax officials. The historian may interest himself in rural administration as part of the life of a particular period, and most readers will find it useful to take note of former administrative arrangements because these still frequently determine how documents are stored, that is, as they were originally collected, in bundles by township or hundred.

In most directories such information was commonly followed by historical notes, mostly on gentlemen's residences and Anglican churches. No comment is offered here on these subjects, beyond the desirability of cross-checking the information against more reliable county and parish histories, notably, where they exist, the parish histories published in *Victoria County Histories*.

Landownership and land use

Kelly 1864:

> Sir Harry Verney, Bart., is lord of the manor; the Hon. Richard Cavendish, and Messrs. William Woolhead, William King, George Wilkinson, Dr Clarke (of Finmere), and Magdalen College, Oxford, are the principal owners. The poor's allotment is 16 acres. There are sand, stone, clay and gravel pits here. The land is arable and pasture, in about equal portions.

Cassey 1865:

> Sir Harry Verney, Bart., is lord of the manor; the Hon. Richard Cavendish, and Messrs. William Woolhead, William King, George Wilkinson, Dr Clarke and Magdalen College, Oxford, are the principal owners. The poor's allotment is 16 acres... The soil is mixed. There are sand, stone, clay, and gravel pits here.

General. The most important general point here is that there may have been some copying going on, although it could be said in partial explanation that both directory agents (or was it the same man?) could have got their information from the same source, perhaps the overseer, who had the ratebook.

Land use. The general characteristics of farming could be easily observed by an agent as he went round the countryside, but for accurate agricultural statistics one should refer to the Board of Agriculture Returns, which began in 1867 (some smallholdings were excluded in the first year, 1866).

The poor's allotment at Thornborough remained in use as such until the inter-war period, located inconveniently well away from the village. This land was given to the poor at the time of the enclosure award (1798) in somewhat ungenerous recompense for loss of common rights and was called an allotment because that term was used by enclosure commissioners for all the new fields, that is, allotments to owners. Only in the middle of the nineteenth century did the term allotment come to have the modern meaning.

As to quarrying, it should be appreciated that many small pits reported in Victorian times were those allotted by enclosure commissioners for the upkeep of the parish highways. Theoretically, their ownership passed to the county councils in the 1890s, and they can sometimes still be identified as dumps for gravel or road salt, though many such places have been created by road realignments. The existence in Thornborough of a brickworks points to the clay pit having had commercial significance. On geology and soils, reference should be made to drift geological and soil maps, probably held by your county library.

Manors. A manorial lord was a person with rights in land other than what we would now call ownership, although he would also actually own some land as well. Where copyhold (customary tenancies) had survived, as in Thornborough, the manor courts were the only means of establishing one's right to inherit a tenancy. With the final conversion in 1926 of remaining copyhold to freehold, the need for these courts disappeared, but the medieval titles are still bought and sold.

Whilst these directories give the firm impression that Sir Harry Verney was the only manorial lord in Thornborough, alternative sources, such as the *Victoria County History*, show that this was not so. Beware, therefore, of incomplete information under this head. However, do not assume that all houses known as Manor House or Manor Farm are reliable indications of the existence of former manors in the legal sense being discussed here. One manor could have been represented by several different houses over the centuries, or indeed by none at all, the court having been held in a convenient inn, like *The Speech House* in the Forest of Dean. Moreover, the English propensity to revere ancient landed titles unfortunately means that there are many spurious manor houses too.

Where there was a single or only one significant manor in a township, it was not unusual for the latter to be referred to as a lordship, especially in the eighteenth and early nineteenth century.

Landownership. The problem of incomplete information also applies here, since directory publishers were not concerned with small owners: after all, many of them would not buy copies of the directories. Among alternative and more reliable sources of information on landownership and land occupancy are some mentioned below, in the Epilogue.

Summary. The tendency of directories to give incomplete information on landownership is well illustrated by the fact that, whilst Thornborough contained 50 landowners according to the 1831 land tax assessment, by 1864–65 this number appears to have gone down to a mere seven, or eight with the poor's allotment. Long experience of the mid-nineteenth-century land market suggests that this is implausible. A much more plausible interpretation is that the directory publishers found lists of 50 owners (by no means exceptional in land tax assessments) too long to handle. Therefore, we can say that directories are much more reliable for the closed townships, which only had a handful of owners, than for the open townships, although hints such as 'and many small proprietors' sometimes occur after the few names given.

Religion

Kelly 1848:

The vicarage, valued at £130 per annum, is held by the Rev. Daniel Watkins. The Wesleyans and Huntingtonians have each a chapel here.

Craven and Musson 1853:

...a vicarage, valued at £130, in the incumbency of the Rev. Daniel Watkins, MA. St Mary's Church. Service, 2 and 6 pm. The Independents and Wesleyans have chapels here. Independent Chapel, no stated minister. Service, 2 and 6 pm. Wesleyan Chapel – circuit preachers. Service, 2 and 6 pm.

Kelly 1864:

The living is a vicarage, valued at £158 per annum, in the gift of Sir Harry Verney, and held by the Rev. Daniel Watkins, of Christ's College, Brecon.

General. These entries suggest that more attention was paid to the established church than to the nonconformist places of worship, but it must be remembered that many of the latter did not have resident clergy, whilst the Clergy Lists, and Crockford's Clerical Directories from 1858, gave the directory publishers an easy way of updating the names of Anglican parsons, as did the Medical Lists in the case of doctors.

Patron of the living. For all manner of historical reasons, many Anglican clergy were not appointed by the bishop of their diocese, but by other establishment figures, mostly lay landowners, but sometimes other clerics and sometimes institutions, such as London livery companies and Oxford and Cambridge colleges. Again many of these patrons were also manorial lords in the parishes where they possessed an advowson, the right to present incumbents to the living. This tradition was in keeping with the medieval and early modern system of preferment through family and personal connections.

Rectory, vicarage. When used in the directories, these terms are not direct references to parsons' dwellings, and would be used even where there was no parsonage house at all. Instead, they are references to the status of the living, the rectors, on the whole being better off than the vicars. This is because far back in the middle ages many livings had been split between a rector (usually a monastic house) and a vicar, with the latter having only the use of the minor portion of the parochial income. At the Dissolution of the Monasteries most separate rectorial rights passed to laymen, along with other monastic property. These owners, also known as lay impropriators of the tithe, were responsible for the upkeep of chancels, but they are not usually identified in directories.

Curates. It was within the powers of an incumbent, whether a rector or a vicar, to appoint a curate to assist him in his duties, and traditionally this was often because the incumbent himself lived miles away from his parish, leaving the curate to do all the work. The curate was appointed at the pleasure of the incumbent, whereas the latter enjoyed the 'parson's freehold', or security of tenure in all but exceptional circumstances. About the beginning of the 'directory period' the Church was busy persuading the parties concerned to adopt a policy of a 'gentleman in every parish'. In principle there were to be no more plural livings (two or more parishes held simultaneously) and instead a commitment to living in the single parish to which the incumbent was appointed. The directories recorded residence of clergy, curates included, in their gentry lists, whilst historical notes often contain details of new parsonage houses, erected to popularise the new policy. (See also above, p.70).

Perpetual curacies. These were one of the stratagems used by the Church to combat nonconformity and to cope with changes in the distribution of population, particularly in the growing urban areas, without creating new parish posts in the old styles. Perpetual curacies were in the gift of bishops and had better conditions of service than the older form of curacy. Some were found in rural areas, especially where land reclamation had, or would have, placed too great a strain on the old parochial system. For example, White's *Directory of Lincolnshire* for 1856 shows that seven new parochial townships had been formed out of the East, West and Wildmore Fens, first drained and settled in 1812. The Rev. Thomas Mitchinson, for instance, was perpetual curate of both Carrington and Frithville, living at the former place, with incomes of £86 and £82 respectively.

Chapelry, chapel-of-ease. Townships that were not also parishes might sometimes contain a place of worship subsidiary to the parish church, known as a chapel-of-ease, and not to be confused with nonconformist chapels. Some of these concessions to long Sunday walks dated back to the Middle Ages, but the growth of rural population in the nineteenth century saw many more built, a process urged on by the evangelical revival of the period. For example, Ballidon in Derbyshire was described by Kelly in 1928 as a small village (population in 1921, 92), township and chapelry in the parish of Bradbourne. The chapel is described as dating back to Norman times, but was thoroughly restored in 1882–83. The living was a chapelry, annexed to the vicarage of Bradbourne, joint net yearly value £210, in the gift of the Duke of Devonshire.

Parish clerk. The name of the clerk may appear in either the descriptive section of a village entry or the list of residents. It was very much a part-time job, generally unpaid. With the separation of church and state at the parish level in the 1890s, this post was replaced by the secretaryship of the Parochial Church Council and the clerkship of the Parish Council.

Nonconformist places of worship. Their history is much less well recorded than that of the established church, though historians of the different denominations have done much in recent years to remedy this inequality. Directories are, therefore, a good starting point for nonconformist history, but need checking against other evidence. For 1851, the Religious Census gives a comprehensive picture of all denominations in all settlements, and is usually available in county record offices, occasionally in a printed form. Evidence on the ground is also helpful, but many chapels were makeshift affairs, and some denominations met in private houses (hence the term 'meeting house', used especially by the Quakers). In Thornborough, the Wesleyan chapel was still in use in the 1980s, the Congregational (Independent) Chapel was a private house, but where the Huntingtonians met is not clear.

Other descriptive material

Many other subjects are reported upon, especially in later directories, this being partly because life became more complex. Charities, postal services, carriers and schools are among the more common subjects, but others include types of employment, country seats, and amenities such as reading rooms, burial grounds (when the churchyards filled up), friendly societies, and traditional events like village feasts and sports. Of these various subjects, it is possible that only charities and schools need any explanation.

Charities. These can be checked at county record offices through the returns made by Clerks of the Peace (of each county) to Parliament (a form of registration), or alternatively in the printed reports of the Charities Commission.

Schools. The local historian needs to be aware of the existence of four main types down to 1902:

1. Those founded by private benefactors and maintained by them and by public subscription. There were a few rural grammar schools in this category, examples being Appleby Magna Free School, Leicestershire, founded and endowed by Sir John Moore in 1627 (*White's Directory*, 1856) and that at Courteenhall, Northamptonshire, founded by Sir Samuel Jones, who was buried in the church nearby in 1672 (*Kelly's Directory*, 1931). A very different kind of private school were those run for commercial profit, the most common manifestation in rural areas being dame schools.

2. British Schools, set up under the British and Foreign School Society, a nonconformist-inspired organisation established in 1810. Its name was a misnomer in the local context, and may have resulted in Anglican retaliation in 1811. Think of these as nonconformist schools and include them with schools named more straightforwardly, for example, as 'Wesleyan' schools.

3.   National Schools, like that at Thornborough, were established under the guidance of the National Society for the Education of the Poor in the Principles of the Established Church set up in 1811. At this date it took over schools established by the Society for the Promotion of Christian Knowledge (SPCK), which were mostly in towns. Note the confusing use of the term 'national' (like 'public' in public schools) and think of these as church schools, like those labelled 'Church of England' schools.

4.   Board Schools. Although other categories of schools had long received government grants, these were the first state schools in England and Wales, the Boards being set up in the wake of the 1870 Education Act which made education compulsory. Where there were no schools, or where existing schools could not get up to the required standards, School Boards were set up covering *ad hoc* districts, sometimes as small as one parish, under the general supervision of the Board of Education in London.

Under the 1902 Education Act, the county and county borough councils (and some smaller boroughs as 'Excepted Districts') became responsible for village schools, which almost all remained as elementary schools for children aged 5–14 until the Education Act of 1944. Under the county junior scholarship schemes, from 1902 increasing numbers of village children transferred at 10 or 11 to grammar schools, preponderantly located in towns, hitherto very largely the preserve of fee-payers. Soon after the 1939–45 war this system was replaced by the eleven-plus exams, and selection continued in force in most areas until the 1960s. During the inter-war period a relatively small number of senior schools for the 11–14 age groups were opened, to which village children could transfer, a few of these schools being located in large villages. These schools became the secondary modern schools after the war and took children on to their fifteenth birthdays, and by the mid-1960s all village children were transferring to secondary schools of some kind. Meanwhile, however, the Victorian system of denominational involvement in the running of schools largely funded by the state has continued in many places, and this applies particularly to village primary schools.

Epilogue: where next?

It may be helpful to conclude with a few remarks on the choice of some other sources, to which the reader can turn to fill out the picture of a community in the 'directory period'. Since directories list only a small fraction of even the adult men of a rural community, it might be most appropriate to turn next to the following sources:

Census Enumerators' Books, familiar to family historians, these give personal details of the whole population at the censuses every tenth year from 1841 to 1891. Under the 100-year rule, details from the 1901 census will be available from January 2002. They are available on microfilm in many central libraries and county record offices. As a massive amount of data is contained in each census — several items on every person — some thought must be given to selecting a particular census for initial study. It is best not to chose the 1841 census as the starting point, as this census gives less detail.[2]

Tithe Surveys and Awards were drawn up under the Tithe Commutation Act in the period from the late 1830s to the mid 1850s. They exist for many parishes, although they do not always cover the whole area. As Tithe Surveys list occupiers as well as owners, it is possible to link them with the 1841 or 1851 census as well as with directories. Plans have generally survived, usually on a scale large enough to show individual dwellings. Consult your county record office.[3]

Land Tax Assessments are also useful on the ownership and occupation of property, but the series surviving in large quantities in record offices generally end at 1832.[4]

1910 Domesday. Unfortunately, the twentieth-century historian is less well supplied with sources of the kinds so far mentioned, but many record offices have copies of the so-called 1910 Domesday. This gives particulars of owners and occupiers of property at that date collected in connection with the introduction of Estate Duty. For many parishes there are accompanying Ordnance Survey 25-inch maps marked up with information.[5]

Rural District Council and Parish Council Minutes. Between the wars a national survey was carried out in respect of housing conditions, and the results for some rural areas have found their way into reference libraries and record offices. Rural District Councils were involved in the introduction of 'urban' amenities to villages, including improvements in sanitation, piped water supplies, refuse collection and the provision of council housing and village halls. These activities were recorded in the minutes of RDCs and Parish Councils, many of which survive, in record offices in the first case, and usually in their respective parishes in the second case. It was only after the passing of the Town and Country Planning Act in 1946 that a significant quantity of planning data and documents was generated.

NOTES

1. Mills, *Lord and peasant*, contains a detailed discussion.
2. For general guidance see Higgs, *Making sense* and *A clearer sense*; and Mills and Schürer, *Local communities*.
3. See Kain and Prince, *Tithe surveys*.
4. On this subject see Gibson and others, *Land and window tax assessments*.
5. See Short, 'Lloyd George "Domesday"'.

BIBLIOGRAPHY AND FURTHER READING

Directories provide an excellent introduction to local history in its widest sense. Readers not already familiar with the sources and methods of local and community history would find it useful to move on to some reading in one of several general books giving guidance over many aspects of the subject. A sample of such titles, marked by a single asterisk, can be found in the bibliography below. Titles marked by two asterisks are recommended in connection with the use of directories in urban areas.

Place of publication is London, except where otherwise stated.

Alexander, D., *Retailing in England during the industrial revolution*, (1970).

Arnold, J., *The Shell book of country crafts*, (1968).

Beckwith, I., *Victorian village*, (Roxby, Lincolnshire WEA, 1967).

Benson, J., *The rise of consumer society in Britain 1880–1980*, (1994).

**Benson, J. *et al.*, 'Sources for the study of urban retailing, 1800–1950, with particular reference to Wolverhampton', *Local Hostorian*, 29 (1999), 167–82. (Listed here for comprehensive introduction to sources).

Benson, J. and Shaw, G. eds., *The evolution of retailing systems, c. 1800–1914*, (Leicester, 1992).

Bracey, H.A., *English rural life: village activities, organisations and institutions*, (1959). Deals mainly with the then contemporary scene, but is very useful all the same.

Chartres, J.A., 'Country tradesmen', and

Chartres, J.A. and Turnbull, G.L., 'Country craftsmen', in Mingay ed., *Victorian countryside*, I, 300–13 and 314–28.

Chartres, J.A., 'Country trades, crafts and professions', Section III of Chapter 5, in Mingay ed., *Agrarian history, VI*, 416–66.

Collins, E.J.T., 'Introduction to Chapter 5, The agricultural servicing and processing industries', in Mingay ed., *Agrarian history, VI*.

**Corfield, P.J. with S. Kelly, '"Giving directions to the town": the early town directories', in R. Rodger ed., *Urban History Yearbook 1984*, (Leicester, 1984), 22–35.

Cracknell, S., 'Nottinghamshire country carriers in the late nineteenth century', *Transactions of the Thoroton Society of Nottinghamshire*, 88 (1984), 76–88.

Crompton, C.A., 'Changes in rural service occupations during the nineteenth century: an evaluation of two sources for Hertfordshire, England', *Rural History*, 6 (1995),192–203.

Crompton, C.A., 'Nineteenth-century craftsmen and tradesmen in Hertfordshire: a spatial, economic and social study of self-sufficiency', (Unpublished Ph.D. thesis, Open University, 1995).

Crompton, C.A., 'An exploration of the craft and trade structure of two Hertfordshire villages, 1851–1891: an application of nominal record linkage to directories and census enumerators' books', *Local Historian*, 28 (1998), 145–58.

Daunton, M.J., *Royal Mail: the Post Office since 1840*, (1984).

Dixon, J., 'Lucas Bemrose's diary of accounts', *Lincolnshire Family History Magazine*, 11, 3 (2000), 155–68.

Drake, M. et al., *Getting into community history*, (Local Population Studies Society, 1995), copies from Dr D.A. Gatley, 114 Thornton Rd, Stoke-on-Trent, ST4 2BD, £2.50 including post and packing (make out cheques to the Society).

**Duggan, E.P., 'Industrialisation and the development of urban business communities: research problems, sources and techniques', *Local Historian*, 11 (1974), 457–65.

Edgar, M.J.D., 'Occupational diversity in seven rural parishes in Dorset in 1851', *Local Population Studies*, 52 (1994), 48–54.

Everitt, A. ed., *Perspectives in English urban history*, (1973), for the chapter entitled 'Town and country in Victorian Leicestershire: the role of the village carrier', 213–40.

Everitt, A., 'Country carriers in the nineteenth century', *Journal of Transport History*, New Series, 3 (1976), 179–202.

Gibson, J., Medlycott, M. and Mills, D. eds, *Land and window tax assessments*, (Federation of Family History Societies, 1993, revised edn of next item).

Gibson, J. and Mills, D. eds, *Land tax assessments, 1690–1950*, (Federation of Family History Societies, 1983).

Goose, N., 'Pubs, inns and beershops: the retail liquor trade in St Albans in the mid-19th century', *Hertfordshire's Past*, 43/4 (1998), 55–60.

Greening, A., 'Nineteenth-century country carriers in north Wiltshire', *Wiltshire Archaeological and Natural History Magazine*, 66 (1971), 162–76.

Hallas, C., 'Craft occupations in the late nineteenth century: some local considerations', *Local Population Studies*, 44 (1990), 18–29. Relates to Swaledale and Wensleydale. Reprinted in Mills and Schürer eds, *Local communities*, 171–83.

Havinden, M.A. *et al.*, *Estate villages: a study of the Berkshire villages of Ardington and Lockinge*, (1966). The classic study of its subject, including sections on non-agricultural occupations.

Haydon, E.S., 'Recording history for the future: Widworthy's occupations in 1992', *Devon and Cornwall Notes and Queries*, 37, III (1993), 87–90.

Hayfield, C., 'Blacksmiths and blacksmiths' shops of the Yorkshire Wolds: a case study of the Wharram area', in Tyska, D. *et al.* eds, *Land, People and Landscapes, essays on the history of the Lincolnshire region*, (Lincoln, 1991), 179–92.

*Hey, D., *Family history and local history in England*, (Harlow, 1987).

Higgs, E., *Making sense of the census. The manuscript returns for England and Wales, 1801–1901*, (1989).

Higgs, E., *A clearer sense of the census. The Victorian censuses and historical research*, (1996).

Holderness, B.A., 'Rural tradesmen, 1660–1850 – a regional study in Lindsey', *Lincolnshire History and Archaeology*, 7 (1972), 77–83. Based on household inventories excepting the later period, for which *White's Directory of Lincolnshire* for 1842 was used.

Jennings, P., *The living village*, (1968).

Jennings, P., 'Occupations in the nineteenth century censuses: the drink retailers of Bradford, West Yorkshire', *Local Population Studies*, 64, (2000), 23–37.

Kain, R.J.P. and Prince, H.C., *Tithe surveys for historians*, (Chichester, 2000).

Law, C.M., 'The growth of urban population in England and Wales, 1801–1911', *Transactions of the Institute of British Geographers*, 41, (1967), 125–43.

Lawton, R., 'Rural depopulation in nineteenth century Britain', reprinted in Mills ed., *English rural communities*, 195–220.

**Lewis, C.R., 'Trade directories – a data source in urban analysis', *National Library of Wales Journal*, 19 (1975), 181–93.

Mackelworth, R., 'Trades, crafts and credit in a Victorian village: a trading family in Milford, Surrey, 1851–1881', *Family and Community History*, 2 (1999), 33–44. Based on the records of a blacksmithing firm that diversified over the period.

Mills, D.R. ed., *English rural communities: the impact of a specialised economy,* (1973).

Mills, D.R., *Lord and peasant in nineteenth century Britain,* (1980).

Mills, D. and J., 'Occupation and social stratification revisited: the census enumerators' books of Victorian England', in R. Rodger ed., *Urban History Yearbook 1989,* (Leicester, 1989), 63–77. Makes use of directory entries in conjunction with census data.

*Mills, D. and Schürer, K. eds, *Local communities in the Victorian census enumerators' books,* (Oxford, 1996).

Mills, D.R., 'Trouble with farms at the Census Office: an evaluation of farm statistics from the censuses of 1851–1881 in England and Wales', *Agricultural History Review,* 47, I (1999), 58–77.

Mingay, G.E. ed., *The Victorian countryside,* 2 vols, (1981).

Mingay, G.E. ed., *The agrarian history of England and Wales, volume VI, 1750–1850,* (Cambridge, 1989).

Moreau, R.E., *The departed village: Berrick Salome at the turn of the century,* (Oxford, 1968). A study of an Oxfordshire village, with good chapters on trades/craftsmen, and on communications, including carriers and postal facilities, *circa* 1900.

Morgan, K., *Country carriers in the Bristol region in the late nineteenth century,* (Bristol, 1986).

**Norton, J.E., *Guide to the national and provincial directories of England and Wales, excluding London, published before 1856,* (Royal Historical Society, 1950).

Obelkevich, J., *Religion and rural society: south Lindsey 1825–1975* (Oxford, 1976).

*Open University, Course DA301 (1994), *Studying family and community history: 19th and 20th centuries,* published by Cambridge University Press in four volumes:

Volume 1, R. Finnegan and M. Drake eds, *From family tree to family history.*

Volume 2, W.T.R. Pryce ed., *From family history to community history.*

Volume 3, J. Golby ed., *Communities and families.*

Volume 4, M. Drake and R. Finnegan eds, *Sources and methods: a handbook.*

**Page, D., 'Commercial directories and market towns', *Local Historian,* 11 (1974), 85–88.

**Raven, N., 'Industry and the small town in Derbyshire: evidence from trade directories, c.1790–1850, in J. Stobart and P. Lane, eds, *Urban and industrial change: the Midlands 1700–1840*, (Leicester, 2000).

Reed, M. and Wells, R. eds, *Class, conflict and protest in the English countryside 1700–1800*, (1990).

Reeves, M., *Sheep bell and ploughshare: the story of two village families*, (Moonraker Press, 1978, 2nd edn, Granada, 1980).

Richardson, J., *The local historian's encyclopedia*, (New Barnet, 1974, and subsequent editions).

*Riden, P., *Local history: a handbook for beginners*, (Batsford, 1983 — 2nd and fully revised edn, Merton Priory Press, 1998).

Robin, J., *Elmdon: continuity and change in a north-west Essex village, 1861–1964*, (Cambridge, 1980). Chapter 6 discusses non-farming occupations.

*Rogers, A., *Approaches to local history*, (Longman, 1977, 1st edn published as *This was their world*, BBC, 1972).

Rose, W., *The village carpenter*, (Cambridge, 1937, reprinted Wakefield, 1973 and London, 1986)

Rose, W., *Good neighbours: some recollections of an English village and its people*, (Cambridge, 1942). Relates to Haddenham, Bucks, and has an excellent chapter on trades/craftsmen.

Saville, J., *Rural depopulation in England and Wales 1851–1951*, (1957).

**Shaw, G., 'The content and reliability of nineteenth-century trade directories', *Local Historian*, 13 (1979), 205–09.

Shaw, G., *British directories as sources in historical geography*, (Norwich, 1982).

Shaw, G. and Tipper, A., *British directories: a bibliography and guide to directories published in England and Wales (1850–1950) and Scotland (1773–1950)*, (Leicester, 1988).

**Shaw, G. and Coles, T., 'European directories: a universal source for urban historians', *Urban History*, 22 (1995), 85–102.

Short, B., 'Local demographic studies of Edwardian England and Wales: the use of the Lloyd George "Domesday" of landownership', *Local Population Studies*, 51 (Autumn 1993), 62–72.

Sturt, G. The wheelwright's shop, (Cambridge, 1923, various reprints).

Sturt, G., *A small boy in the sixties*, (Cambridge, 1932).

Summer, M., 'Tradesmen of Hook Norton in the nineteenth century', *Cake and Cockhorse*, 9 (1983), 74–78.

*Tiller, K., *English local history: an introduction*, (Stroud, 1992).

**Timmins, G., 'Measuring industrial growth from trade directories', *Local Historian*, 13 (1979), 349–52.

Tupling, G.H., *Lancashire directories 1684–1957*, (Manchester, 1968, edn revised by S. Horrocks).

Weekley, I., 'Lateral interdependence as an aspect of rural service provision: a Northamptonshire case study', *East Midland Geographer*, 6 (1977), 361–74. Although concerned with the contemporary situation, this is a seminal paper on village interdependence.

*West, J., *Village records*, (2nd edn Chichester, 1962).

**Wilde, P., 'The use of business directories in comparing the industrial structure of towns: an example from the south-west Pennines, *Local Historian*, 12 (1976), 152–56.

*Williams, M.A., *Researching local history: the human journey*, (1996).

Wymer, N., *English country crafts: a survey of their development from early times to present day*, (1946).

SUBJECT INDEX

Subject index

Subject index

Subject index

Subject index